SLACK WATER

MONA MUDD

Mona Mudd ♡

Orange Hat Publishing
www.orangehatpublishing.com - Waukesha, WI

For Will and Maggie
And for the guy in the seat behind me

"All streams flow to the sea,
Yet the sea is never full.
To the place the streams come from,
There they return again."
~ Ecclesiastes 1:7

~ Witness, January 2013

I was born in the village of Mildenhall on the Royal Air Force base at Lakenheath in England in 1974 to Ray and Connie Chevalier. We returned to the States in 1978, and in 1979, my parents divorced. My dad was transferred to the South Pacific and, though my memory may have failed me, I can't remember seeing him for many years after that. My mom and I returned to St. Louis, Missouri, to be near her family, and I began kindergarten at St. Mary's School in Bridgeton, Missouri. St. Mary's Parish, the streets where we lived, our neighborhood market, my childhood home . . . all of them are long gone. Demolished in 1989 for the irreparable slight of being too close to progress.

They say you can't go home again and, well, I suppose that's about as true as anything else they've ever said.

Hi. My name is Mona Mudd.

INTRODUCTION
present day

In January 2012, I was chosen as the director of a spiritual retreat at my parish. Before I allow you to imagine that this was a distinction based on merit, let me assure you it was not. Those on the discernment team later communicated to me that I was chosen throughout the process for my similarities to St. Peter, who did not want to lead, did not feel qualified to lead, nor felt worthy of the honor. Still, it seemed to me a poor choice at the time. I have no lust for power. No desire to be the one setting the best example.

However, chosen I was, and as I fulfilled the obligations of the role, it became clear that the role of leader was simply assigned from an organizational capacity, not based on any significant or necessary talent on my end. Anyone who has ever been thrust into the eyes of leadership knows that you lead from behind, you rally the troops, and if there is trouble to be had, it is yours to shoulder. As the old adage goes, "God does not call the qualified. He qualifies the called." So it came to pass that for only the time I needed, I did the best I was able to do. As I was called to do it quite a few times after that, I have to assume my best was good enough.

One facet of my role was to write what religious people call a Witness. A Witness is just what it sounds like: a witness to faith in the world, the Church in the world. *Witness,* as a verb, is defined as "to have knowledge of an event of change from personal observation or experience." *Witness,* as a noun, is a document which professes that this is the faith I have witnessed in the world. The director of this retreat writes the Witness based upon her own experience.

The rules surrounding this Witness were few, in order to let the Holy Spirit do most of the work, but they were inflexible. They numbered three:

1. The Witness must be twenty to thirty minutes in length, spoken.
2. The Witness must incorporate Scripture, which, I have to be honest, was a bit obvious to me. It was a religious retreat after all.
3. It must center around the topic the writer has been assigned. My topic was Discipleship.

This was a daunting task to me. Not the idea of *Discipleship.* The topic, it was of little interest to me. The Holy Spirit is the greatest storyteller there is, so He would do the work of revealing through me the reality of *Discipleship* to those who attended the retreat.

No, what was daunting was that there were so many stories to tell. How do I confine them to a stopwatch? Thirty minutes to tell a story isn't much. Thirty minutes to tell a story from scratch. Thirty minutes to tell a story to a roomful of strangers and #bytheway—be inspiring if you can manage it.

I think it's a challenge—a fear—we will all one day face in its final form: When the hour comes when we are all given a limited amount of time, what will be the story you have told with your life? The you in the shadows, led only by your fears? Or the you in the light? Will you tell a story of fear or one of courage? Which story, as I was called to tell one, would be more authentic and useful to another soul on her search?

The Unformed Me was the obvious answer. Nobody is inspired by a person whose essential message is: *Look how amazing I am*. It is only our common brokenness that opens us to grace. It is our flaws which are heroic, not our accomplishments.

But which one? The Unformed Me that I admit? The one whose fears and follies are acceptable, sometimes even kind of slapdash and funny? Or the one I keep hidden? Because that's much harder for me to expose. To leave myself vulnerable, unformed, unprotected in the raw daylight. And that's going to be hard for you too.

Do I tell the story of that summer? That summer of 2008. The summer I put everything down and walked right out of my life. Perhaps an ill-fitting solution, to use a Band-Aid to cover a massive wound, but I—we—needed to breathe. I will tell you that I left my children for eight out of ten weeks that summer, and you won't like that part. That's okay, nobody likes that part. Because we want to connect, you and I. Even now, as young as our relationship is, you want me to be someone to you. You want me to be someone whose motives look familiar to you. Someone understandable. Someone likeable. Someone forgivable.

This Witness was also a daunting task because there would be many who appear nowhere between its pages who made untold contributions toward the gift of someone I can be proud of. And there would be many who were exceedingly unkind, yet ultimately meaningless, who for whatever reason would have a published role in the final credits of this one act.

My friend David was old money in Chicago. His father was a surgeon—an oncologist, I believe. He lived in Chicago all his life until he met Misa in his late twenties. Misa and David married and eventually moved to Providence, Rhode Island. Misa was the director of a summer camp on Cape Cod in Brewster, Massachusetts, where I worked from 2008 until 2012. It was through her that I met her husband David.

David once took me to task over a little summer attraction I had. He felt that I should behave differently. I remember him saying, "This is all fun for you, but you're going to leave. You're *leaving*, Mona," he repeated. "And he has to live here. He has to watch you leave."

I remember that I got mad and accused him of being overly dramatic. In my experience, there are thousands of people on this planet more memorable and valuable than me. At the time, David and I were standing in the office of a summer camp on *Cape Cod*, for heaven's sake! You can't tell me that any number of the people who live on or land on Cape Cod in the summer aren't more fascinating than one girl from North County in Missouri. I told him as much, then I turned to get back to work. But I could feel him still looking at me.

"*What?*" Frustrated, I spun my chair back to face him.

He studied me for a moment with a clinical expression, one which surely would have made his father proud, before he came to his decision about me.

"You underestimate your effect on people, Monamudd."

I was insulted by the surety with which he spoke, the calm arrogance of the accusation, but before I could even react, he added, "I bet that's your greatest flaw."

Do I? Is it? It was unnerving. Only one other person in my life had ever assessed the reality of me so confidently, so succinctly.

I am assigning more meaning to that moment in hindsight than I did at the time. At the time, I spun back to my computer, shoved away the thought and him with it. But over time, it began to occur to me what he meant. To overestimate your value to others is at best foolish, an unfortunate little vanity to behold. But to underestimate your value to others wreaks a sad havoc of its own.

I was sitting in the backyard one night with my friend, Dan. A chilly night, under a green, striped lawn umbrella, we sat as we so often do. He, in his Adirondack chair with his feet on another chair. Me, in my own chair with my toes toasty on the side of his leg. A position of practicality, mostly. (The mosquitoes in Missouri are no joke for your ankles.) But also one of comfort and warmth, a careless intimacy we think nothing of in the moment. Dan always smells of rye and tobacco to me. A lifelong smoker, and yet he has never smelled of cigarette smoke. Instead a rustier, earthier smell lingers if you get close enough to know.

"I need something else," I was complaining. "I love teaching, but I need something else."

To fill the coffers was our current conversation. As a Catholic school teacher, worry over finances assaults me at regular intervals. Too stubborn I am, and too proud to ask for help. Plus, I'm a bit of a fraud as a teacher. I see people on social media who read books about education in their spare time, and I always think to myself, *I would never in a million years do that on my summer break* (or during the school year either, if you must know the truth).

My friend Cathy teases me that I only became a teacher because I couldn't become a talk show host. She says a classroom is the only place in the real world where I can stand up in front of a crowd and "polish my act." *Thank you, thank you. I'll be here all week.*

"You. Should. Write." This from Dan as he swatted at a mosquito in the backyard. He is frustrated by the number of times he needs to encourage me down this particular path.

"Oh, *wriiiiite . . .*" I said. People suggest that as if it's so easy when, in reality, the path from here to there is a fluid, luckless journey that I haven't the resources nor the connections to navigate. Write. *Pah!* As if a story tells itself.

"I can't just write *anything*," I said.

"Why not?"

"All I ever write about is myself! It's the only thing I know how to write about. The world doesn't care about that."

"No," he countered. "You *think* you only write about yourself. That's what you tell people, that's what you tell me, that's what you tell yourself because you're just writing your own thoughts. But you write about parenting and families . . . you write about teaching, about faith . . . you actually write about a lot of stuff."

I dismissed the idea. "You always say that."

He threw his hands in the air, a quick snap of annoyed surrender.

The conversation ended. The impossibility of it reaffirmed in my mind. But later, it came back to me. *A story,* I thought, *such a nebulous thing.* To pick one, virtually impossible in the length of a lifetime. What is teased forward? What is forgiven, what is lost? Given the limited attention span of culture, through which lens do you tell the story that mattered the most?

I had scoffed at Dan—a mental *Pah!* all artistic temperament. *As if a story writes itself.*

But what if it's already written? The question met me three days later in the shower, of all places. What if I had been writing it for a decade?

The thread unraveled, all grace and form, a fishing line on a sunlit sea. Words, like dominoes, how they *clickety-clacked* through my memories. Words already written—*tumbletumbletumble*—they rolled around my mind.

In my haste, I towel-dried enough to get by. I threw on my robe, careful to not disturb the precarious nature of the thoughts unfolding. Neither too far forward nor too far back would do. Never to be disturbed, nor frozen or memorized. Words. They can only be held while in flight.

I veered around the upstairs corner. Slipping a little on my damp feet, I grabbed the railing and thundered down the stairs in search of my laptop.

"*Shhhh*!" I commanded Will when I rounded the corner into the kitchen. He was leaning against the counter eating cereal at whatever passes as a college kid's breakfast hour. He looked up from his phone.

"O . . . kay?"

It was preventative. Words spoken aloud in that moment would have torn the lacy, delicate fabric of the ones forming in my mind. I grabbed the laptop, careful to unplug the cord, and shouldered past Maggie on my way back up the stairs.

"Say nothing!" I commanded as she drew breath to speak.

"I HAVE AN IDEA!" I shouted on my way past her on the landing, as if this explained the erraticism of my behavior. But in its way, and to my children, it did.

In the shower, I had remembered something. I remembered those questions, the very same ones I asked myself so long ago in preparation of my Witness. I remembered that though the questions were complex and numerous, the answers were simple. The *answer*—singular—was simple, and I knew it all along.

One single thing, and it's the *only* thing: a good story wants to be told.

Tell it.

*"Thy word is a lamp unto my feet
and a light unto my path."
~ Psalm 119:105*

~ *Witness, January 2013*

One of my favorite things to do in life is to lose myself in a good book. A good story, I should say. I have no need for some impersonal collection of facts. Give me a myth. Give me a legend. I have just finished reading a book called Isle of Palms *by Dorothea Benton Frank. The main character of the book, Anna, had been forced to move away from this particular island off the coast of South Carolina as a child, but she could not forget the sense of belonging she felt when she was there. As an adult, Anna returned to the* Isle of Palms, *and from that point on, her life was perfectly marvelous. There was a bit more to it than that, but that's the story arc in a nutshell. At any rate, it struck a chord with me— this idea that you could belong to a place and it to you. It was an idea that I had never put into words myself, but one I recognized as the truth as soon as I read it.*

For as long as I can remember, my dad has lived on the East Coast. When I was ten years old, he got remarried to a woman named Shelley. Shelley's family was a prominent one in a small town in Maryland, and every year they rented an enormous house on any beach along the Eastern seaboard and took their family vacation together. The very first of these trips that I attended with my dad and his new extended family was in Delaware. As soon as we pulled into the driveway, Shelley swung open the door and leapt out of the car.

"Leave everything here!" she commanded. "I'm not letting you do anything until you've seen the ocean!" I couldn't imagine what the big deal was. I had seen pictures of the ocean, for heaven's sake. I may have been landlocked, but I didn't live in a bubble.

She grabbed my hand and towed me forward—down the driveway, past the house (it was on stilts!), over the sand dunes—

And there I stopped.

Nothing in my life had prepared me for that first glimpse of the Atlantic Ocean. I could see the ocean, yes, but more than that I could feel it. Here was this heaving, churning, living thing that rose and fell. Rose and fell. It was magnificent to me. Maybe it's because life had always struck me that way. Beautiful. Turbulent. Eternal.

From that point on, we went to the beach nearly every year that I came to visit. I loved the area with its particular brand of energy and its grainy beaches more and more with every visit. I loved my dad. And I loved my stepmother. They became who I wanted to become.

When Dad and Shelley divorced ten years later, it was a blow that I did not see coming and one that devastated me. And although I don't claim to have felt the blow as keenly as them, or as keenly as my half-brother and half-sister must have felt it, it was not an event I recovered from quickly or easily.

Later that same year, my stepdad was laid off when his company downsized, and he and my mom moved to Chicago. Not long after that, I became pregnant with my son. Will's father left town when Will was nine months old, and life took on a different shape for me. I stopped seeing Dad. I stopped seeing the ocean. Life *was more concrete. I was more concerned with day-to-day living and working, far away from abstract thoughts of the ocean and the idea that a part of me belonged there. As the years passed, I diminished my feelings as people tend to do when they are denied something they truly desire. A childhood flight of fancy, I thought. If I thought of it at all.*

I worked at Sam's Club unloading tractor-trailers to pay my way through night school. Kindness wasn't really necessary to the job. I had friends, of course, but I wouldn't have classified myself at that time as a particularly friendly person. While working there, I met and married a fellow coworker. He was nice enough, hysterically funny, but he was quite cynical. Nothing was sacred. He made fun of church. He made fun of God. And so did I.

One day, I was standing on my forklift waiting for another driver to pass, and I somehow became aware of myself in a new way. It was a quiet moment, bound by nothing, when I inexplicably saw my own reflection. How had I become so callous, so scabbed over? I looked around and saw the harshness and fatigue in the lives and on the faces of so many of my coworkers, and though I wouldn't judge them—because I was definitely one of them—I knew that they weren't me. That their lives weren't mine.

It was a random Sunday, in a random year, when I decided to return to church. I walked in, and I promise you that I heard in my heart, "Welcome back." It was Palm Sunday.

"Crucify Him. Crucify Him." I cried all the way through it.

CHAPTER ONE

2014

"Autobiography in Five Short Chapters"
by Portia Nelson

Chapter One

I walk down the street.
There is a deep hole in the sidewalk.
I fall in.
I am lost . . . I am helpless.
It isn't my fault.
It takes forever to find a way out.

1.

slack water

As I sit here at our home away from home on Cape Cod, I am taking some time to myself. There are footsteps upstairs. David is going in and out the screen door getting ready to go fishing. The clatter of my typing is working in harmony with the hollow echo of the wooden screen door opening and slamming. Opening and slamming. A dropped spool of fishing line. The scratch of Velcro being pulled apart. It's quite a lovely bit of music.

I have a lunch date with one of my very best friends soon. I have already dropped Maggie off at her first day of camp. I still have to go to the grocery store. But for now, I want to sit for a moment and write.

Maggie's first day of camp was—well, there's nothing else to call it except a joyous affair! From Susie, who commands the parking lot every morning and spied us first, to all of the calls of "Hello!" and "Welcome back!" and every moment in between. It was magical! The heady elixir of pure summer.

Summer camp brings us all back together, and the love at ours is a palpable thing. Yes, of course there is love at home too. We see it every day. But this is the celebratory kind that rejoices in changes, even as we breathe a sigh of relief that everything is also still the same. The camp songs are the same. The same people are in the office. The same faces are brought back into focus after ten months apart. It is the joy of reunions, and it is impossible to describe or replace.

Maggie's counselor this year is a young woman named Shannon. A new face, but one whose spirit instantly made me feel my daughter was in good hands.

I said to her, "Hi! I'm Mona Mudd. My daughter Maggie Mudd is a Laser this year." Instantly, she knew who she was. "Oh . . . Maggie *Mudd*!" she said and looked around for her.

"She's still over there." I pointed toward the wooden benches by the art tent. Maggie, much like me, had made her way into camp calling greetings and giving hugs to familiar friends and staff.

"Oh, Maggie Muuuuudd . . ." Shannon stretched out the name. "We have been waiting for her! I have been asked so many times when she was getting here that I couldn't *wait* to find out who she was!"

"Did you think she'd float in on a cloud?" I joked.

Watching her progress across the campus, her counselor affirmed, "I actually think she kind of did!"

After dropping Maggie off, I came home to my inaugural "long and lonely"—which is the name Misa termed years ago to describe my long walks on the beach alone. My walks aren't as long as they used to be, nor are they as lonely. But when I first arrived here, they were.

In 2008, for my first summer here, I—well, I don't want to say I was *lost*. That's trite, it's so very maudlin. But I was wandering on a strange path, perhaps as lost as I was found. I call it my "slack water" phase. Slack water—which used to be called the "stand of tide"—is defined by Google as "a short period in a tidal body of water when the water has no rise and no fall." Before every turn of the tide, there is a time of *slack water*.

I like that visual because, while the surface may appear listless or still, underneath, a massive shift is preparing to take place. *The tide is turning*, and while that is such a simple phrase, one we are all so familiar with that it seems ordinary, it is forever and always anything but ordinary. Imagine how massive that shift actually is. The tide is *turning*. Every drop of water in the ocean is preparing to move in a different direction. Can you imagine the forces that must be at work for that to happen? And it is no less monumental when we—as people— attempt to overhaul ourselves. Never underestimate the power of a person determined to change.

So, this summer. This *first* summer. It was my time of slack water. When the tide of myself was preparing to turn. And every year when I come back and take my first long and lonely, I can't help but mark my distance from it, like a child marking their growth on a wall. No matter what becomes of me, and of this place, and of these people, and—perhaps generations down the line—whatever happens to these roads, or this camp, or this sandbar we call Cape Cod, it will always be the place which gave me the space I needed to turn around.

While Misa lives in Rhode Island currently, she was raised on the Cape where Marcia, her mother, still lives. Marcia hosts a reunion every couple of years for the staff of the former camp she used to run in the early '70s. Her current house, in fact, sits upon the land of that bygone campground. At this reunion, they reenact one of their old camp traditions, and during one of my early summers, I took part.

We walked the path down to the bay one night. A path which I would come to know by heart all the summers that followed. Its pitches and ruts, the homes nearby only revealed in peeks and glimpses through the thick groves of swaying trees. Up a gentle rise, veer down and to the left. At the end of the path, the grass begins to thin and the sand begins.

Once we rounded a small boathouse, the moonlit bay came into view and each of us was given a candle to set adrift on the water. I studied it, not sure what their hope for the activity was. I could see that the candle was rendered temporarily buoyant by the cup shape of the wax-coated filter surrounding it, but at the time, I was so in my head that I'm not sure I was paying all that much attention to anything else. But somehow I knew that what I held in my hand was important. It was as important as anything else. It was a wish. It was a hope. And there was somehow magic in it. I don't know if I did it right . . . I don't even know if it was right to think of myself. Maybe I was supposed to send hope out to the world. Maybe I was supposed to be grateful for what I had. Maybe I was supposed to just hope like hell the candles didn't set the dock on fire. But I did the only thing I could think of: I gave my troubles to the sea, and I promised to come back.

So, every summer we return. Partly because we are in love with this part of our life. Partly because I promised I would. We hug old friends. Cherish long-missed faces. Linger in the company of those too long gone from our lives. We buy "penny candy" at the Brewster Store. Eat a meal at Cobie's. Get ice cream at Kate's Seafood & Ice Cream. Maybe we'll sneak in a new memory or two.

We will spend time on the bay beach where there is absolutely no cell signal and nothing to take us away from the moment. Our faces are chapped by the wind and browned by the sun. We will sleep every night in a house with the windows open, the fans on, and the frogs croaking in the distance. And always, *always* the distant thrum of the surf. And this year will be no different. I know that. I am immeasurably grateful for that.

But every year—before all that happens—I walk again the path to the sea. I have never forgotten my promise. At the shore, I stop and put my hands in the water and I tell the water that I have come back. I remember that long ago night when, desperate, I gave my troubles to the sea, and I return to honor the sea for keeping them.

2.

stealing time

Last night, I talked to my friend Cathy on the phone for a bit. Or—to be specific—we talked for *exactly* six minutes before I had to leave for Home Visit. Cath took the lead:

> *"What is going on over there?! You are in the choir now? Since when?"*
> Me: *"I just started a few weeks ago! I love it!"*
> Cath: *"That doesn't even sound like a thing. It sounds like a bad alibi. There's a reason the police say, 'He's no choir boy,' when they have a bunch of suspects!"*

This is why I love Cathy. She is one part sister and one part heckler. She is the strongest, most wonderfully supportive person you'll ever know. She is my anchor. My boots on the ground.

When I was going through a custody battle and was growing increasingly paranoid as a result of the deposition questions, I called her in a panic:

> Me: *"One of them is 'Do I have a private investigator?' Do you think he does?! What if someone's watching me, Cath?!"*

Cath: "Please. You go to work. Go to church. Go to your mom's. And spend time with your kids. If someone was watching you, they wouldn't write a report, they'd fall asleep."

Or when a guy named John broke my heart, I left a teary message on her voicemail. She called back and left me a message:

"MONA. You cannot leave me a message like that and then not pick up the phone. Is your head in the oven?? I'm hanging up and calling back. PICK UP THE PHONE!"

She is the person who unfailingly makes me laugh at myself and also puts the highs and lows of my life into a more manageable context so it doesn't feel so unwieldy to me.

Cath and her husband are in the middle of moving to Texas. This is a situation which finds her very preoccupied with eating the "heavy food."

"Girl, did you know that you have to pay for your cross-country moving truck by the pound?! Every time John asks me what I want for dinner, I tell him, "We don't need to eat the crackers—they're lightweight. We need to eat that heavy-ass bag of rice and all the food in cans!"

This is a bittersweet move for her, as it also is for me. Though not for the same reasons. It's not that I will miss her, geographically speaking. She moved away from St. Louis a long time ago. It is just—for me—another change in the rolling transition my life has become. With Cathy's move, and with my house for sale, and especially with Will leaving for college, I am more sensitive to the passage of time lately. The winds of change which blow unceasingly.

My friend, Marcia, read a passage from a book to me a few months ago on the phone, and, while I am going to get this wrong, I will try to pass along the crux of the passage. It said something like, "If you want time to go by faster, then grow older. Because yesterday was New Year's Day. Today is Christmas. Tomorrow will be five years from now." And I'm not old. I'm not saying that. But *time*. It goes by so quickly.

A friend of mine once told me that God's voice is everywhere. He said, "Say you are considering getting a cat, but you're not sure if you should. God's voice is in the ad on the pub wall: *Help wanted: Caterpillar machinery driver.* It's in the cat food ad on the side of the bus. It's in the friend who turns to wave goodbye to her friend Cathy and says, 'Bye, Cat!'"

It's in the things you can see if you are willing to see them. And that was the first time I had ever heard my experience of God's voice explained so well.

It so happened that during my first summer on the Cape, Cathy was grieving the loss of her mother and she was a shattered shell of herself. There is no other way to describe the consuming grief she endured. On the floor. Broken.

Into my solitary world that summer kept entering Cathy and her grief. All I can remember of our conversations during that period of our lives was her saying over and over, "*Time . . . time . . .* if I had only had more time with her . . . if I only could have had more time to tell her how much I loved her."

Cathy's mother died with no business undone between them. While she lived, there was no time lost. Still, in the end. *Time.* There is never enough of it. It was God's voice in Cathy's grief. Cathy reminding me of the preciousness of *time* was God bringing some infinitesimal grace out of heartbreak. I missed my children in my skin that summer. In my cells. In my bones.

My sorrow in their absence leaked out of me everywhere. Tears, unbidden, poured forth in such a way that wasn't even crying so much as it was a perpetual draining. I had sprung a leak. I never had experienced that depth of sorrow before. Here I was, a mother without her children, faced with a child who had just lost her mother.

There was a moment one day early in the summer when my friend Misa said to me, "Monamudd, we love having you here. We do. And I know it is with considerable heartache you have come. But you are here now, and if you want to go . . . *go*. Go home with all our love and blessings."

She took my hands. "But might I suggest you stay. *Stay*. Take the water, the sun, the ocean air and consider healing yourself first. Then go home and heal Will and Maggie."

In that moment—heart-to-heart, my hands in hers, more tears in the sand—I believe God's voice was in Misa's voice as much as it was in Cathy's.

Six minutes later, I got off the phone with Cathy. Then Maggie and I drove down to my Aunt Mary's house. This week is our family's "Home Visit." Home Visit is a four (sometimes five!) day affair when my aunt, Sister Stephanie, gets to come home from the convent and stay with us.

These four days are lovely in their own way. We get to see Sr. Stephanie, of course. I get to see my far-flung cousins: John comes in from China, and Carrie is in from Los Angeles with her beautiful daughter. Plus, I get to see the cousins I have in town but don't see that often. And the food! The food is so constant and plentiful that it borders on gluttony.

Last week . . .
Bill: "Why are you guys eating right before dinner?"
Mom: "Home Visit is coming up—we have to be prepared
to eat even when we're not hungry."
Me: "We're not eating, Bill! We're weight training!"

But even Home Visit—a constant in my life since before I can remember—carries with it change. Naturally, I think the changes are most notable to Sr. Stephanie. A year has gone by. We are all a little different. Edges might be softened . . . or sharpened, depending on the year. The babies are bigger. Some are away at college this year. Some are home again. Yesterday's children are today's mothers and fathers. Time works its magic in a million ways on all of us.

I noticed this year, more than anything else, the change in Maggie. Last year she was a little girl. We all turned around and she changed. It's in how she interacts with adults. Speaks to them, looks them in the eye, takes the hand of a younger cousin, remembers her manners.

Suddenly, the young lady she will become is visible beneath the surface. And though none of us can stop time—and none of us would really want to—her change was, in its own way, as bittersweet as Will leaving for college. She needs to take these steps forward, just as her brother needs to take his. Even as we celebrate the progress, we mourn a bit the loss, don't we?

When I was a little girl—and I wish Maggie and Will were here to hear this story. Maggie because she loves the magical world of the me-before-her. Will because he knew his great-grandma and grandpa. Anyway, we lived in a house with an attic fan.

Now, it was not always on. My grandmother found it too loud and intrusive a sound. But sometimes on Indian summer days, she found it desirable to coax the air of a darkening evening into a mite-too-stuffy house and she would give me the all clear.

"Honey," she would call from the family room. "Go turn on the attic fan."

And how I would *rush* to the switch, as if she would change her mind. The heavy *whoosh* of the opening vents was a celebration to me, as were the few that were dust-stuck for a heartbeat before finally opening. Instantly, a tide of air bowled ass-over-elbow in through the screens, a sudden influx of air that invariably slammed an unsuspecting door somewhere else in the house.

I'd watch her lace curtains billow, sometimes stuck pressed to the screen and sometimes dancing about. And oh how I wished I could fall asleep fast to the sound of the fan with the diagonal splash of light from her room painted across my bedtime covers. And sometimes I did, but mostly I didn't. The attic fan was inevitably silenced. The lights turned off. The house quieted. The attic fan was replaced by the lower, fainter, somehow less important sound of her fan by her bed.

These were my favorite moments . . . I don't even really know why. The heavy noise, the rattle of slats, the seldomness of the event. It was a treat. A memory in the making. To this day, in my memory, I can still hear her call, "*Honey . . .*" in the heavy *whoosh* of our own attic fan.

Maggie fell asleep in my bed last night (not totally grown up yet!), and as I locked up the house for the night, I remembered how Will and Maggie, each in their own times, used to crawl into my bed in the morning and we'd talk. Will stopped doing it so long ago that I don't even remember the last time. For Maggie, it has gone by the wayside more recently as she found more and more reasons to greet the day without me (television, an uncompleted craft, desire for her own quiet time before the day began). But I would have to say mostly it was just the nature of living that separated our experience of the morning. I wake up early, and she doesn't anymore. We lived our way out of those moments. As I crawled into bed last night, I found myself missing them, wishing those moments back in some small, vague way.

Yet, I have always loved the beauty of time passing. The glorious cyclical nature of it. I love seasons. I love books which are dynastic in nature. Books about generations of families. Sagas. How one generation rolls into the next fascinates me. Time takes away, perhaps, but it also gives. It gives of its very self so that we can *be*. So that we can live, love, and experience. Time only takes what it gave in the first place. Even as I mourn its passing, I respect it. I am inspired by it.

Three o'clock in the morning rolled around and found us both awake. Maggie and me. The covers were crooked. Someone used the restroom. Maybe both of us. But there we were. Awake. Facing each other.

She told me about her dream. I told her what she looked like when she was dreaming (she's a lively sleeper). She giggled. I laughed. The cat cuddled on the bed. The blower of the A/C kicked on, reminding me faintly of my own distant memories. Somewhere in the distance, a police siren rolled by. We whispered some more. A train thundered through town.

Her eyes took on a faraway expression. "The train . . ." she whispered.

I said, "Do you know that one day when you don't live by the train tracks anymore, you will—out of nowhere—catch the sound of a train. And you will say to your own daughter,

'One night, when I was a little girl, I woke up in the middle of the night . . .'"

She said, ". . . and my mom had a terrible cold . . ."

I laughed at her awareness of me. "Yes, you will say, *'And Nana had a terrible cold . . .'* because I will be their Nana."

She giggled at the very idea.

"And you will say, *'We snuggled in bed, and it was so* rainy *that summer. And we talked about our day and giggled about the cat . . .'"*

"I'll probably have to stop and tell them about Chloe . . ."

"Oh, definitely! And do you know that that is how wonderful memories are? That the poor, high, lonesome sound of a train years and years from now will bring you right back to this room, with all these pillows, and these walls . . . and right back into this moment."

"Hmmmm . . . I love that," she said, and then:

"Mommy, look . . ." and I knew she was getting sleepy again. These days, she only calls me *Mommy* when she's too tired to remember that she's growing up.

"Mommy, look. I'm in the perfect place right here with you." Soon, she closed her eyes. But just before she fell back to sleep, she reached out, and I took her hand in mine, and I got a little bit of time back.

Today, time will march on again. Yes it will. And tomorrow will be next week. And Cathy will find her house in Dallas. I will switch jobs. I will sell my house. We will find a new home base. Yes, Will is moving on. Yes, Maggie is growing up.

And while yesterday reminded me of all the moving on we're all doing, this very early morning reminded me that there are different types of time. There is the overarching time attributed to families and generations. And there are moments of time between people. On the phone. At home. At three o'clock in the morning. And there is the elastic time attributed to memories. Those sun-splashed sunset leftover pieces of time that we get to keep.

My cousins and I were remembering Grandma and Grandpa yesterday. We shared so many wonderful memories of them as we sat around the family room. The stories waned, and my cousin, Annie, said into the silence that followed, "I still miss her so much . . ." And I miss him. We all miss both of them. It is a fitting tribute to time gone by.

The story of my family's life is told through our memories of Grandma and Grandpa. It is told in the generations that have come after them. It is told in the memories that will follow us.

It is lived out around swimming pools. On the back deck of a house in Shrewsbury. In the flower garden at Mom's. It is told in the collective journeys we've taken and in all the times we've come back home. It is illustrated in a small child on a hip, a line of people waiting to fill their plates with supper, a baby being fed in my cousin's lap. A lively conversation around a summer table. A laugh. A hug. A smile. A long goodbye on the front walk. Families tell the story of time, and they tell it so well.

Every grandchild in my family has a quilt made up of the pieces of childhood t-shirts. My grandma used to make them, and now my mom does. The shirts are remembered, memories revisited, and then pieced back together as an object to bring comfort. Warmth. Mom is getting ready to begin one for Cathy made out of her dad's shirts. With time marches along comfort as well. Will's comforter used to be on his bed. Now it is in the linen closet. He meant to take it to college and forgot.

But isn't that the passage of time in a nutshell? No matter how hard we try, some things we forget. Like the quilts, sometimes it is put away. Sometimes it is forgotten. Sometimes we celebrate it: a birth, a graduation. Sometimes we mourn it. Sometimes it is too heavy. But always, *always* it can be brought back out and remembered, bringing comfort and warmth. While lately I am extra conscious of time's passing, I can't regret what the passing of it continues to give to me: births, joys, and journeys. Hearth fires in the winter. The glory of a summer afternoon.

Someone said to me on my fortieth birthday, "It's all downhill from here!"

Is it? I don't think so. I look around me, and I see so much joy in time's passing and an abundance of life to come. We can't slow down time, but we can slow down ourselves. And what Maggie's hand in mine reminded me at three o'clock this morning was just that: No, I can't stop time. But in the middle of the night—when the world around me is fast asleep—my girl and I can *steal* it.

3.

a bunny's wake

I have long shaken my head at classrooms on television. As if teachers ever actually get the opportunity to talk without being interrupted. As if students ever sit quietly and soak up the cherished wisdom of their elders. It makes me laugh (because crying would be such a waste of time) that Hollywood imagines that is how modern classrooms operate: eyes on the teacher, not a single person out of place. Even distractions are low-key and charming: passing a note, glancing at a friend, a harmless comment spoken with no lingering follow-up. With Hollywood passing this peacefulness off as a classroom, well, it's no wonder people believe teaching is so easy that anybody can do it.

But, Life has thrown me a blessing that I have done nothing really to deserve other than being in the right place at the right time, and it is that this year I found myself accepting a job in a private independent school that actually *does* fit the Hollywood definition of school. Can you imagine such a place? The mind boggles. A garden on campus. An emphasis on music and art and movement that is not just talked about, but encouraged and implemented. I can hardly believe my good fortune. Suspicious person that I am, I find myself with a lingering *waiting for the other shoe to drop* type of feeling. Like I'm not a lucky enough person to deserve this. But. Be that as it may, I know I am blessed, and I hope to have the good grace to remember that.

At our school, there is a strong experiential learning component that finds the middle school grades on a trip every September to parts of the country with different experiences of life. These differences are scientific in nature on the surface: different topography, geography, or climate. But the impact of these differences creates such a profound effect on the culture of a place that we also find ourselves experiencing a completely different lifestyle with every new trip.

These trips fall primarily under the science curriculum. One is a trip to Nova Scotia. No. Not Nova Scotia—I always say that, but it's actually New Brunswick. Near Nova Scotia, but not. We travel with the students to Maine and then from there into Canada to the Huntsman Marine Science Centre Program on the Bay of Fundy in St. Andrews, New Brunswick. This trip introduces the students to marine biology through experiences on the water and in the classroom and on the windy beaches of this gorgeous, but rather desolate place. It is an incredible experience, for all of us really. One that none of us, students and teachers alike, are likely to forget.

Another trip, in another year, takes us west to Cortez, Colorado, near Mesa Verde to the Crow Canyon Archeological Center. We stay on-site in their dorms. While there, we learn about past cultures—again, in the classroom and in the field. The students visit real archaeological sites and spend time with graduate students doing fieldwork, with American Indians working to also preserve their ways of life. The students get to clean actual artifacts! I can remember a moment in the lab, holding a pottery shard from a dig, and being blown away that the last person who touched this—this piece of a buried way of life that I was holding in my hand—lived nine hundred years ago. Just me and that person lost in time. Still, to this day, I can hardly wrap my mind around that.

Now, these trips, thrilling as they may be, also have a component of hilarity that only exists in certain circumstances. You see, you have to remember that our Head of School and I are with a class of fifth and sixth graders for five or six days straight. Inspired though they may be, they are exhausted. They go from morning until night. They are busy, but a little homesick. They are babies, really. Away from Mom and Dad and the comfort they provide. Away from parents who—in some cases—never have even taught them how to make a bed or pour their own cereal.

In light of that, there are a lot of moments that grow their souls, which is such a beautiful transformation to witness, but it also creates some difficult moments to walk them through. As such, the Head of School, Sam, and I are profoundly exhausted by the tail end of this trip.

So, this last trip. The one to Colorado. We have taught them to be on time, to make their beds, to follow directions in a strange land. We have hiked to the cliff dwellings of Mesa Verde in the hot, hot Colorado sun. We have worked in the lab, toured museums, made braids with twine. We have taught them to make fire using teamwork and a piece of leather, a rock, a stick, and a bow. We have played games that the American Indians played. We have practiced shooting a bow and arrow. We have overseen teeth-brushing, bedtime, breakfast, lunch, and dinner for five. straight. days. And it is our *last day*.

We are touring, by bus, a few of the active archaeological digs in Mesa Verde National Park. It is hot. The students have been eating food that has not been made-to-order for close to a week by this point. Breakfast, lunch, and dinner. They are wiped out, bone-dry. But they are troopers. They are the sweetest kids and so polite. It is only their innate politeness as a community that keeps their eyes on the tour guide, even though we can see that they have shut it off. They have hit the limit of the knowledge they wish to possess on this subject.

And suddenly into this moment, though they try to remember their manners, I can see that their attention has been snagged by something.

Click, click. It starts. It has stolen their attention from the tour guide like the new kid in school steals attention from an old favorite. Some of them are pointing. Covertly, of course. Their manners wouldn't have them be obvious with their inattention. The pictures . . . oh, those cameras are whirring and clicking. The tour guide is asking questions, but no one is answering. They are a class possessed, enchanted even, by this one thing that is intriguing. This one small thing that has become the only thing they care to process: There is a dead rabbit on the floor of the archaeological site.

Recent. Freshly deceased. And it is *captivating*.

Sam and I have been on this trip for five days as well. What is an educational experience for our students becomes for us an endurance test, and we spend 100% of our time navigating a class of mildly displaced pre-teens.

And Sam and I? We build endurance through laughter. Sam and I have long succumbed to the giggles about everything. We are barely holding it together enough to be good examples to our sweet, sweet charges. Everything is hysterical. The kids. Their problems. Their reactions. Their demands. ("I want REAL FOOD!") In fact, it's been about twenty-four hours since Sam and I decided by a mutual agreement that we can no longer make eye contact with each other.

Noticing this dead rabbit, I stroll over to Sam. I stand next to her at the railing that keeps us from tumbling down into this site and sharing this poor bunny's fate. I stand there for a minute. Timing is everything, you know.

I make a production of standing on my tiptoes. Peering, child-like, fascinated, over the edge. And then I say to her, in a low voice, "*Gosh.*"

She bows her head a bit—movement is a great strategy for fending off hilarity. Just a shuffle of feet. A rolling of the shoulders, a clearing of the throat. Any other little thing for the mind to focus upon will do the trick because she knows. She knows *exactly* what I'm going to say.

I look around. "This site is *really well-preserved*, isn't it?"

I hear a sharp little intake of breath. Like that moment when you are trying to organize your mouth, or lips, or your teeth in such a way that a laugh will (for pity's sake!) stay inside.

"I mean, look at that rabbit," I gestured down into the hole, ". . . that thing looks like it just died yesterday!"

And I thought I was going to be able to pull it off. I did.

I had been warming up the joke for a while, so I thought I had built up the tolerance required to say it. But, no.

The tour guide droned on. The kids? They were still great. So attentive, such charmers.

But the chaperones?

Notsomuch.

4.

the boys of fall

It's time.

I know it is because I heard it on the radio while I was driving to work yesterday: "The Boys of Fall."

When I feel that chill, smell that fresh cut grass
I'm back in my helmet, cleats, and shoulder pads
Standing in the huddle, listening to the call
Fans going crazy for the boys of fall

This is a song by Kenny Chesney which our local DJs actually use for something rather sweet. Every Friday, they give a shout-out to all the local high schools who have a football game that night—all the "Friday Night Lights" games, they call them. And they play this song, "The Boys of Fall," and intersperse it with people—parents and students—who have called in to say good luck to their sons or their friends:

"Good luck, Francis Howell Vikings!"

"Good luck, Gavin, who's playing tonight at Fort Zumwalt North!"

As the season progresses, so do the well-wishes for students, and sons, and friends who are moving on to District Finals, or Regionals, or the State Championship. We do this every Friday morning, and it's adorable.

It's sweet. It's local. It's all the tiny moments that our memories are made of in the first place. It touches the part of all of us that is forever young. I was a cheerleader in high school (State Champs ourselves, three years running thankyouverymuch), so I have a thousand memories of being on the sidelines under those Friday night lights. These well-wishes are our collective youth, encapsulated.

There are so many things I love about the Midwest, and I don't say them often enough. If spring is the kickoff to my summer, my Cape Cod, my summer camp, my time with my beautiful, *beautiful* friends on the coast. My inspiration. My big picture...

Then fall—and football season—is the kickoff (quite literally) to every single moment which makes the big picture even matter: childhood friends, pumpkin carving, bonfires, book reports, and football games. Christmas lights. Church bells. Little conversations with other teachers in the doorways of our classrooms before we begin our day. Dinner with Mom and Bill. Phone calls from friends. These are the things that knit my life together and make inspiration even *possible.*

One of my friends, Marcia, who lives in Massachusetts, once told me that her son briefly dated a woman who was from . . . Arizona? Maybe? Somewhere out West. She didn't have much to say about this nameless woman, save that, "This was the first time we had ever become aware of this phenomenon out West . . . this deep loyalty to their college football team." She went on, "And every year they go back . . .

and they pile into the stadium, and they go crazy for it. Every year! It is phenomenal!"

Marcia is one of the very few people I know who—when faced with something entirely different from herself—is 100% delighted by it. She has an unquenchable desire to experience the diversity of life. She has a master's degree from Harvard, and she admitted to me that this "Western phenomenon" was about as far away as you could get from "tea and harmonicas under a tent at Harvard."

She said, "I would just love to *see* it one day! I can't even wrap my mind around it!"

I told her that it was, in fact, indescribable. To which she added, "They do it in the *Mid*west too?! I had no idea it was so widespread!"

I told her that every year I have had the opportunity to fly down to my friends in Dallas, and we attend the annual Red River Rivalry game between Oklahoma University and the University of Texas.

It is a game that takes place at the Cotton Bowl in the middle of the Texas County Fair. It is hot. It is a mass of humanity. You can eat more fried food than you ever wanted to *think* about (Oreos, a Thanksgiving dinner, beer, etc.). You walk all day long. People are shouting. People are riding Ferris wheels . . . they're looking at cars . . . you can buy a rooster. It is massive in every way: physically, psychologically, mentally, emotionally. And it is a weekend to which I affectionately refer—to anyone who will listen—as, "The most fun weekend I have ALL YEAR!"

I didn't go away to college. I had my son at barely twenty-one years old and attended ten years of night school to get my degree, so I never had the college experience. Honestly, I don't feel that I particularly mourn the loss of it—being a bit of a homebody—but I absolutely celebrate my chance to enjoy the fruits of somebody else's labor every year. Someone *else* went to college there . . . that's good enough for me!

Cathy's husband, John, and his friend Eric went to Oklahoma University back in the day. If my friend Cathy is a "Sooner by marriage"—as she says—then I am simply a "Sooner by association." I'm simply there. Every year. Buying the fried beer (not really).

Every year, Eric and John sit in the good seats, with the cool crowd. And every year, Cath and I sit up in the cheap seats with a slightly rowdier crowd. A rowdiness that we may or may not contribute to by forcing everyone around us—OU and UT fans alike—to be our friends.

In short, Eric and John are down at the fifty-yard line where people are wearing polos and khaki pants, but Cath and I are up where they are wearing war paint and standing on the metal bleachers, giving high fives to all the fanatics around us.

From these years, I have accumulated more OU Sooner paraphernalia than anyone has a right to, considering I've barely even set foot on Oklahoma soil. But that is not the point. The point is that this is something that has become as much a part of me as my own memories.

This game. This place. These people. This weekend. This experience.

Truly, with as much time as I spend pitching my eyes to the northeast, it is as much a delight as it is a surprise to find so much feeling and joy to the south and west. But that's me. I'm often completely unaware of what's right in front of me.

But when they play that song on the radio, I can see it. When the nights start to get chilly, I can feel it. If I listen really hard,

I can hear it. The roar of the stadium. The crush of the crowd. When the school year starts and I pass my days in the classroom drinking coffee out of the OU mug one of my students gave me last year, I can feel that they're almost here: the boys of fall.

Stephen Fry, an Englishman, has a six-part BBC television series in which he travels across the United States. Just before he was born, his father was offered a job at Princeton University in New Jersey, but turned it down in favor of a position in England. Perhaps this accounts for Mr. Fry's slight interest in America—the echo of a road not taken, I imagine.

One of his travels took him to Alabama where he attended an Auburn/Alabama game. He says early in the broadcast, as he pans to the crowd gathering, the band warming up, the cameras moving across the field:

"It is an indication of the size of the American economy, and their passion for sport, that this is the stadium of Auburn— no more than a medium-sized college—and their annual game against another college in the same state, the University of Alabama.

"It has the scale, intensity, and hoopla of a Grand National Final but is, in reality, nothing more than a local derby between amateur students." And he sounds cynical, yes. But you can tell that he's reluctantly amazed. I don't think he's impressed. But he is amazed.

They show him laughing at the antics of the marching band. Getting his hand painted by the bare-chested fans, whom he finds remarkably funny. They show him startled by the cheerleaders leaping and being thrown around. We see Mr. Fry surrounded by a stadium filled with people singing "God Bless America"—that for however a rowdy and drunken version it may be—is clearly charming to him.

The final scene is Mr. Fry, teary-eyed at the ending strains of "The Star-Spangled Banner" with a massive American flag waving grandly in the background. And finally. He is impressed.

"I don't know if anything sums up America better," he says as he takes in the chaos, the cheerfulness, the crowd. "It's simultaneously preposterous, incredibly laughable. Charming. Ridiculous and expensive. Overpopulated. Wonderful, America."

5.

straight outta noco

Sometimes . . . on the way home from work on a sunny, cool Tuesday afternoon . . . my mind wanders. And really, it's apt to go anywhere. Long-lost memories from childhood that I try to nudge into clarity. My grocery list. Things I need to remember to do, or to say, or to think about. Anything at all, really. While I drive home, my mind unravels. Many times my mind stumbles across a memory in its entirety and I laugh about it. Out loud. Right there in the middle of my daily commute.

I went to high school with a guy named Dan. Not Dan who sits in the backyard with me. No, this was a different guy named Dan. We'll call him Dan C.

Dan C. and I didn't run with the same crowd, but I thought he was nice enough. Very funny. Pretty wry sense of humor. Caustic, one might say. I had French class with him, I do remember that. And he, along with Dan-who-sits-in-the-backyard-with-me, was extraordinarily trying to our teacher, Mrs. O'Donnell.

Excuse me, *Madame* O'Donnell.

But beyond that, I didn't have a lot of dealings with Dan C.

until my senior year. Even then, I simply enjoyed his company when I came across it. I didn't seek it out. I certainly would never claim we knew each other well.

Now, as it happened, I fell asleep next to Dan on prom night. Before you think that I'm using "fell asleep" as a euphemism, let me tell you that I am not. I fell asleep. Quite literally. It was late. Probably 4 A.M. We all had rooms at the Fairfield Inn off Highway 270. I was tired, and I crawled into an available space and fell asleep. End of story.

I woke up the next day. My girlfriends and I went home. Perhaps you think I have forgotten any euphemistic-worthy activities? I have not. I am not now, nor have I ever been, the kind of person who has vast stretches of memories obliterated by alcohol. I have too many control issues to put my life (and memories) in the hands of such a fickle, tricky mistress.

But that's not why I laughed in the car today.

Running parallel to this . . .

I was friends with this guy named Dave whom I worked with at Cecil Whittaker's Pizza in Florissant. When I first laid eyes on Dave, he was coming in the back door of the restaurant, backlit by the sunset shining behind him. You think I am being hyperbolic, but I am not. He was—honest to God—*backlit*. It was a page straight out of a seventeen-year-old's fantasy playbook. It wasn't too long before Dave and I started dating. We ended up dating for about a year and a half. It was a good eighteen months, broken apart only by "Different Stage of Life Syndrome" which is as sneaky as it is effective. But to this day, I have so many favorite memories of Dave that I am not sure where to start.

About a month after we started dating, Dave broke up with me. As it happened, he was late to work the next day. Angry as I was, I was delighted to be chosen by our boss to go retrieve him. I drove to his house. When I got there, I greeted his parents, who were sitting companionably in the living room drinking coffee and reading the paper. I strode down the steps to find him asleep. In one smooth motion, I yanked the pillow out from under his head and smacked him across the face with it.

"You're LATE!" I yelled. He looked at me and said, "Oh my God, this is a nightmare . . ." I left the way I came, and he arrived at work shortly thereafter.

But that's not why I laughed in the car today.

Perhaps my favorite memory was toward the end of this initial break-up phase. Dave had broken up with his girlfriend, Connie, to date me. Then a month later, he reversed that process. It happened that Connie lived on the road that fed into my friend Julie's street. On the way to Julie's one day, I spotted his truck. Since I had *specifically* asked him if he was going back to her when we broke up, and he had said no, I felt this couldn't pass without a little . . . retribution.

Immediately upon arrival at Julie's house, I began paging him. Oh . . . I guess about every five minutes. For an hour. He never called me back. Clearly. Who would? But I laughed about that more than I can say. Julie's whole family was laughing about it. I think we might have actually taken turns dialing the phone during dinner, come to think of it. It was just so comical to us . . . this idea that he was trying to have a romantic reunion and that damn pager on his belt kept going off.

The next day at work, he walked in the back door, and I

turned—my face a mask of purity. Of innocence. How could anybody be mad at this face? He yelled to me from the back of the restaurant to the front counter:

"YOU!"

I stuck my head around the corner to peer back in the kitchen. *"Me?"* I gestured to the phone at my ear. He couldn't talk to me; I was taking a pizza order.

Uncaring, he poked a furious finger at me. *"You're a brat!"* he yelled. "Has anybody ever told you that?! You're a *BRAT*!"

"Okay, that will be there in about forty-five minutes," I said into the phone. And then I couldn't help it—I fell out laughing. Oh! The fun we had with that!

My girlfriend Bridget laughed at him. Our friend Angie was working that day . . . *she* was laughing. I think Julie was there . . . she was still laughing from the night before. Dave told everyone what I did, and got no traction whatsoever.

He complained about that for a solid fifteen minutes. He grabbed the pizza pan and chucked a pizza out of the oven—still yelling. He sliced that poor person's pizza in a rare fury. He regaled us all with his ruined evening, his mislaid plans . . . and he couldn't get any sympathy at all, the poor sap. As a delivery driver, Dave was pretty high up on the pizza place pecking order . . . but the rest of the drivers were laughing at him too. Hell, even the kid who washed the dishes was laughing at him.

It was asinine behavior on my part, and in no world beyond seventeen years of age would (or should) that behavior be applauded. But that day it was hilarious. And that is, I suppose, what I liked about him the most. I was a hot mess. I was way too young to be as complicated as I was. But he somehow knew the balance of how to bear that without fencing it in, or putting it out. He deserves my honor for that. He deserves every good thing his life now holds.

But that's not why I laughed in the car today.

The one thing about Dave that was rather burdensome was that he was a fighter. At the slightest provocation, he'd toss that elbow into somebody's chin. He'd throw a punch if someone looked at me funny. It was ridiculous. It was like dating your bodyguard. I can't tell you how many times I had to stop that fool from getting into a fight in somebody's driveway.

One night, I had just been dropped off by the police at a Denny's in Illinois (*Mom, stay with me. It sounds worse than it was . . .*) because my girlfriends and I had a flat tire. I called Dave from the payphone, and his crazy self was in the hospital getting stitches because he was at a party where someone threw a beer bottle and it broke across his face. I mean . . . *what the hell*? Fool.

But that's not why I laughed in the car today. *Obviously.*

What I laughed about in the car today was an almost forgotten memory. A few months out of high school, Dave and I attended a party at my friend Amy's house. And guess who was there? My old friend, Dan C.

After prom, and as time wore on, I began to piece together that Dan was upset with me about something. One of my friends confessed that Dan was telling people that he and I had been involved in . . . a euphemism . . . on prom night. I will assure you, my memory holds and we were not. But I have always remained wary of the siren song of alcohol. Of oblivion. Even at a young age. And I don't like to accuse a man . . . but let's just say that I'm not sure if he could say the same. Nevertheless, he fancied himself spurned, and I was sorry for that.

It so happened that on the night of this party, he was standing near Dave and me. He was mumbling things just below the level of the conversation. Obscenities. Rude things. Ridiculous comments.

And Dave kept glancing over at him.

"Nobody wants you here . . ."

Dave would look over. He'd look a little nonplussed. Then he'd go back to his conversation.

Knowing Dan kind of liked me and here I was with someone else, I felt bad for him. I turned to Dan and said hello. He nodded. Then, I turned back.

"You don't belong here . . ." he mumbled.

Increasingly nervous, I tried to smile back at him again. *Easy does it. Keep calm.* But I was as nervous as a wet cat . . . I mean, I knew Dan's feelings were hurt by whatever he imagined we might have possibly ever been . . . but I also knew Dave. Dave, who had glanced over at him *again*.

"Yeah, I'm talking to you . . ."

My heart kicked into gear. *Oh dear God . . .*

I grabbed Dave's hand. "Hey," I said. "Just ignore it."

"I am."

"I do not want you to get in a fight over this."

"I don't want to either. This is your friend's house, but if he says one more thi—"

"No!" I said, putting my foot down finally. I was *so sick* of all his fighting. "*No.* Just ignore what he's saying completely. *Please.* He's a nice guy. He doesn't know you. You *do* belong here . . ."

"*Me?*" he yelled. A bit louder than necessary, if you ask me.

"Yes. *Shhh!*" I lowered my voice. "He keeps saying these

things to you ... I think maybe he's been drinking or something? I'm not sure but, h—"

"*ME?*" And he laughed a little bit.

That did it. "YES! *You.* What? Why do you keep saying that!?"

"He's not saying those things to *me.* He's saying them to *you.*"

And *that* was why I laughed in the car today.

6.

assumption

There was a moment today when the shape of my life came into focus. It happens to me sometimes. A brief peek into what my life could be. What I wouldn't have chosen for myself at the outset, but what might choose me in the end.

My children and I have lived in the twin shadows of Assumption Church's steeples for about six years. For six years, we have marked the time by those church bells and watched the sun set behind them. For six years, the bells of Assumption have told us the story of everyone's lives. Every funeral. Every wedding. Every Christmas morning. And every Easter Sunday.

Now, six years is not long in the space of a lifetime. Six years won't get you out of grade school. It won't get you out of your teens. It is barely a blink in the timeline of parenting. But six years is the longest I have been anywhere. And there was a moment—standing in the church's narthex today—when the view out the doors of that place struck me as one of the only things I've ever known by heart.

I didn't choose Assumption Church. In fact, I tried repeatedly to *un*-choose it. When my children and I moved back to O'Fallon, Missouri, I knew enough about myself and my wishes for them that I wanted to find a church for us to attend.

One of the first I attended was Assumption. There was a two-week window between the end of my job in Massachusetts and the beginning of my job in St. Louis. So I used those two weeks to try to find a place to belong. And by belong, I meant that it would belong to us, not that we would belong to it.

To be honest? I don't like commitment. Commitment may one day ask something of me that I don't want to give, so I never put myself in that position. Not anymore. I don't want to be depended on; I don't want to be necessary. But the Mass was fine even if I did feel a little conspicuous. A weekday Mass is not the time to hide in plain sight. I didn't love it. But I didn't *not* love it either.

A day went by. I drove my daughter to preschool. And out my car window, I heard the bells again, the slightly rowdy, joyous pealing of them. After Mass, this woman—who I still see all the time, but to this day don't know her name—stopped and said to me, "I just want you to know that I see you here, and I'm glad you're here." And that kind of freaked me out. So I let some time go by.

My pattern of returning to this church came in fits and starts and was—to be honest—probably rather graceless. Any time I could dodge the priest, I would. I wouldn't make eye contact. I did not make conversation. Do you want to read at Mass? *No, I do not.* Do you want to distribute Communion? *No, thank you.* Do you want to attend a retreat? *Not even a little bit.* I can't explain to you how much I didn't want to be known. But gradually, I came to accept that I was. Somehow in a Sunday crowd of 500 or more, I was.

Years went by. Maggie started kindergarten at Assumption, and her teacher—to me—seemed to know everything about everything. In first grade, her teacher was everything I thought a first-grade teacher should be. By the time Maggie was in second grade, I had recently been hired by the school. I remember on Back-to-School Night feeling so blessed that—although I did not really know any of these teachers from the man on the moon—I could finally be counted among them. Those who I believed then and still believe now to be the best in their fields.

For the next two years, Maggie and I both attended Assumption School. We lived together. Slept in the same house. Woke up. Drove across the street to school . . . where we stayed for the next eight hours in the same building. Then we went home together. And although I still have the rest of my life to live, I will promise you right now that I will forever count those as two of the most divinely lived years of my life.

Last year, I left Assumption. For many reasons. All of them good. All of them necessary. All of them right. But, as I told the vice principal last May, "Assumption has the distinction of being the only place I have ever left, but didn't want to go." *But by the grace of God, go I.* Within that grace, I am blessed to have landed in a sweet, fairy-tale of a place. I shake my head sometimes at the incredible good grace which finds me where I am, with the people I am surrounded by. Time and time again.

My challenge to myself during that bygone time of transition was that I wanted to do this leaving right. It has been my experience that when I let something go, it is gone from my life. Forever. In many ways, I have set things up that way. Time and time again, I have started my life over again from scratch. So it was with an incredible amount of care that I undertook my departure from this place and these people who mattered so much to me.

When Mags and I found ourselves in Assumption Church today, it was to mourn the ultimate loss: the death of a loved one. While my focus was on Grandma Genny and our family, I couldn't escape the realization that death brings so clearly at times. Sometimes loss clarifies what has been found.

After the service and the reception, Maggie and I popped into Assumption during the school day to say hello. What met us at all the doors was an unstoppable tide of belonging and, at some points, an unstoppable tide of people. Maggie was met with hugs and leaps of joy and a clamoring to say hello and ask her how her new school was. And did she miss us? And when are you coming back?

I was greeted with the kind of love and hugs and foolish joy you can really only give your second-grade teacher. I had to check out the haircuts, and the new braces, and look at those sweet faces again, one by one. Oh! How they've grown! At one point, a new boy to Assumption School said, "I don't even know who these people are, and I feel like hugging them!"

Truly, if I gave out one hug, I gave out ninety-five. I got to see my teacher friends and get more love from them than a girl ever did anything to deserve. My favorite moment was from Rose, who treats me with the tenderness I never have the strength to ask for. She framed my face with her hands and said, "Oh, I miss you so much." It was bliss. Such a balm to us both after the sadness of the morning.

It was in those moments I saw that Assumption had chosen me and that I belonged to her. Oh, I may never teach there again. I truly love where I am, and you can't plow a straight line looking back. But—in spite of my best efforts—I have become a part of something. I belong somewhere. I am necessary. I am known.

My friend Cheri and I once served on two back-to-back retreat committees (yes, I eventually attended one . . . then another, and another). At the very end of the second retreat, she and I found ourselves walking down the side stairwell of the church. It was late in the evening. Everyone had gone. The church was quiet, and only a faint yellow glow over a silent crucifix remained.

Cheri remarked that she couldn't believe it was over. That it was hard to let go of the planning, and the coordinating, and the close relationships we had all built with our group throughout it all. She said, "It's just hard. Letting go is hard."

"Is it?" I asked. "I've never found that to be true."

She stopped and looked at me for a heartbeat of a moment, then broke out in a lightning-fast grin and linked my arm tightly with hers.

"Oh, stop it!" She jostled our joined arms a little. "You just want everybody to *think* it's easy for you to let go. But you hold on to people, Monamudd. Oh, I know you now! *You hold on.*"

7.

a cuppa silence

Words. Sometimes it strikes me that words are at once my greatest blessing and my greatest curse. They whir through my mind on a constant basis like the old microfiche files at the library. It could be supposed that the greatest relationship I have in life is with the English language. It soothes me. It is what I am forever in search of creating and receiving. A good turn of phrase or a well-expressed thought are collectables to me. I love to listen to intelligent people speak. Many people find me well-spoken. I don't believe I am . . . I am usually just quoting someone else. But it is a certain gift, I suppose, to keep a cache of quotes or thoughts in your back pocket and give them away as life demands it, or to meet the comforts of those around you.

But, words. They are my constant companion. The pursuit of them in a book. The comfort derived from them when they are used well. The unburdening of them in a journal. They bring humor. They bring peace. They bring a sense of accomplishment. They take me away. But sometimes, they are a burden to me. They take me too far away, and I can't get back to the moment I'm in. On certain days, I exist in a near-constant state of daydreaming. Crafting thoughts. Considering options. Reviewing conversations. *Prev*iewing conversations. Organizing the vast collection of words which I have at my disposal.

It is on those days that I have to rely upon something which I practice for the express purpose of *stopping* that which I usually chase so ardently. The opposite of words. The other half of my life's desire: silence. Not silence around me, for I can rarely command that. But silence within me.

It is why I find myself on those days not listening to music on my walk. Sure, nature contains sounds of life and neighborhoods make noise, but somehow that is outside of me, and I enjoy the lack of noise being directly aimed at my ears.

It is why I find myself in church. It may be simply years of conditioning, but in a church, I find a silence, a profound silence, which eludes me in life and echoes in my heart. I noticed it especially yesterday when my thoughts were quite frantic. Once I dipped my hand in that baptismal font to bless myself upon entering church, it all stopped.

The words of the book *Sylvester and the Magic Pebble* come back to me: "The rain did not gradually taper off. It simply ceased." I am paraphrasing that, of course. But my thoughts went the way of Sylvester's rain in the story. They did not gradually go away. They ceased. Silence greeted me while I was in church. What a blessed relief.

Sally Kempton once said, "It is hard to fight an enemy who has outposts in your head." That is my battle with words. They exist in me. They are beloved by me, and since I love them, I cannot put them from me. But since I do not command them, they often besiege me when I have no need of them.

Finally, that is why I practice meditation. Oh, I do not practice it well. I am fidgety. There is such life to get back to! There are such words to pursue, books to read, writing to do! But I practice it so that I can lay claim to the process of meditation (rudimentary though mine may be) when I need it.

Jane Eyre said to Mr. Rochester:

"I will hold to the principles received by me when I was sane, and not mad—as I am now. Laws and principles are not for the times when there is no temptation: they are for such moments as this, when body and soul rise in mutiny against their rigour . . . If at my individual convenience I might break them, what would be their worth? They have a worth—so I have always believed; and if I cannot believe it now, it is because I am insane—quite insane . . . Preconceived opinions, foregone determinations, are all I have at this hour to stand by: there I plant my foot."

Jane was talking about the fight between reason and passion, all quite a bit more lofty than me just having too many thoughts in my head yesterday. But I always think about that when I feel beyond my ability to arrest my thoughts—that it is to save me from the madness of those moments that I practice all of the others. So that when I get beyond myself, I have the more saner practices in my life to fall back on. The meditation. The faith. The silence.

All of them combined beautifully yesterday to come to my aid, a fact for which I am immeasurably grateful. Even more, I am grateful that I have been blessed with the practice of reaching for them, believing that they will save me if I but believe in their power to do so.

There are things going on in Maggie's life that are burdensome to me. She is not a burden. Never. But the road she must walk is one I have been on, and it makes me sad. I wonder what I can do to help. I cannot take her burden from her . . .

though I would if I could. But I want to make it lighter. I worry if I am capable. Is it enough to be steady? I cannot be what I am not, and I cannot be everything. Am I enough?

I once went to confession, and somehow in the course of it, I found myself just speaking to the priest casually. I said, "I feel so guilty sometimes that I cannot give my children much. That I am not capable of giving them the best in life."

He said, "Do you give them faith to find comfort in?"

I said, "I try."

He said, "Do you give them love?"

I said, "Yes, absolutely."

He said, "Do you give them a home where they can find peace?"

I said, "Yes."

"Well, then I think your burden lies in your definition of the phrase 'the best in life,' because it sounds like that is exactly what you are giving them."

Like a moment of absolute silence or an applicable quote that I pull out at the right time, I am glad I have that moment as well. That I can remind myself that I don't need to adjust myself when I feel burdened or less than ideal as a parent, I need only adjust my definition. Contact with the world and all its charms and possessions can be seductive. It can make us think we are not as valuable as we are.

I spent the whole of yesterday listing for myself what I lack. Telling myself I needed to be better. Somehow more . . . oh, I don't know if I have enough words to actually pinpoint anything. I just had a prevailing feeling that I should just be *more*. Somehow more than I am. Some nebulous and troublesome *more*.

It is in these moments that I know I get lost to myself.

Though it is never easy because I want to close ranks and keep to myself, I know that I need to get outside of myself when I feel this happening. I need to *engage*, not disengage. So I went to Mass . . . and the load was lightened for a while. I went to lunch with Mom . . . and the load began to shift away from me more. Around three o'clock, Mom and I took Will to see the display of our new house . . . and in the process of planning, the load was lightened again.

Finally, we went to see the plot of land which will become our house and our yard, our view and the backdrop to a new chapter of memories. It was in that moment it happened. Quite without any warning, in the middle of an empty field, I came back to myself.

It is not much. Most of the land is common ground, not ours at all. It is filled with mud, brambles, dead leaves, and roots. But there is a certain peace in that spot. A Sunday afternoon quiet that filled in the missing places where words had been. A peace that made Will stand in the middle of it and say, "This is a good spot."

In that moment, I could swear to you I felt the life beneath my feet, sleeping. Just waiting to be lived again. And just like that . . . the words left. In their place was the moment I was in. The persistent squawk of a bird in a tree. The sun and its descent. The air that was colder than I thought when I had left the house without a coat. Mom measuring by paces the dimensions of the lot, and Will moving away to explore beyond it. I stood there, filled with gratitude for the silence that found me.

I am not flashy. I am not perfect. I think children need more than we realize and less than we think. I think they do not need so much hovering, but I think they do need us to play checkers with them. I think they do not need a grand home, but they do need a place to come home to. I think they do not need us to be perfect, but they do need us to be okay with who we are, so that through us they can learn to be okay with who they are.

No, we do not have anything that would be considered excess. We are building a small attached cottage with a postage stamp-sized yard. But I can make it a home. I can fill it with peace and prayer. I can give them a garden in the back and cheerful flower pots on the front porch . . . and a wind chime. Yes, a wind chime out back. To me there is no sweeter sound for a home.

I cannot take them on grand vacations, but I can take them to summer camp.

I cannot give them the world, but I can give them a conversation.

I cannot give them what I don't have. But I can give them what I am.

In the end—and with a little bit of luck—that will be enough.

"Therefore, as the Holy Spirit says, 'Today when you
hear His voice, do not harden your hearts . . .'"
~ Hebrews 3:7

~ Witness, January 2013

The first time I can remember seeing Mary, I was eight years old. I had gone to bed during an argument between my family members. I lived in a house with my mom, my grandma, my grandpa, my uncle, and my aunt. My aunt Katie is one of my favorite people. She was diagnosed in the fifties with what we would likely call an autism spectrum disorder today.

She was the sun around which our family orbited: her needs, her preferences, her dislikes. She was my babysitter, my friend, my eccentric sister. When I was young and my friend Lynn and I disobeyed our parents and watched Friday the 13th anyway, I slept on the floor of Katie's bedroom for a week. She taught me to shave my legs. Then she provided a wad of cotton to roll across the gaping slice on my shin, and we kind of hoped no one would notice. She helped me with homework when she could. She provided, and still provides, our family with more stories of hilarity than all the others of us combined.

But the world was too loud for her, too confusing in its subterfuge and trickery, and she could get angry. In my childhood, she was prone to what doctors called "episodes"—again, these were old-fashioned terms for the behavior. I was sent to my room when she would get angry and begin yelling or crying. To this day, I am not sure if it is more frightening to see someone lose control of herself in person, or to simply hear it on the other side of the bedroom door.

Since these behaviors tended to erupt after dinner, or after my family had wine or gin, it was often bedtime before the storm passed. Mary—or who I came to think of as Mary, as she was dressed in robes—would be there in the very early morning hours when I awoke to realize the crisis had passed. I would open my eyes, and there she would be, over in the corner by the hanging lamp in my room. Terrified, I would pinch my eyes shut, count to ten, and open them again to find her gone. I don't know if it was a figment of my imagination, though I would like to think that if it was, I would have had enough sense to conjure something that was comforting to me rather than something that scared me half to death.

Alcohol was the seventh member of our family and the one who took up the most space. There were many nights I would wake to hear Grandma falling out of the kitchen chair. I would attempt to help, but my aunt Katie would always come out of her room— awakened by the noise as well—and block me. I can still see her hand and the way it would block me from stepping out of my room. My grandpa once notably fell out of the shower, shattering the shower door on his way down. But these events do not define them as a whole. They do not tell you how patient Grandma was in teaching me to sew, to bake apple pies, or what a fabulous and gusty Irish laugh she had. They do not tell you that every day, my grandpa picked me up from school and talked to me about my day as he cooked dinner. That he let me paint ceramics with him, that he watched The Facts of Life with me every day at four o'clock.

There was a lot of love and laughter, I feel honor bound to

point that out, but the extremes were difficult to navigate. And therein lay the beauty and the difficulty of being raised in that house.

I only had one friend. Her name was Lynn, and she lived down the street from me. Her family had the same basic dynamic. Very much love and laughter. Very much togetherness. But in both houses, there was rather an array of troubles. Someone was drinking. Someone drove into a ditch. Someone was in jail. It seemed to be never-ending, and that it appeared to not affect our relative happiness seems absurd to suggest. Sure, it did. It must have affected the way we perceived the world. I know that. But what I recall overwhelmingly from childhood is Lynn and our friendship and our time together. Lynn and I have often spoken of the past, and we have concluded that what saved us was the fact that it was the same in both houses. We were not spared the environment, no. But we were spared the shame that could have come with it had there been an alternate comparison to draw. What saved us was each other.

Mom hit rock bottom the night before my twelfth birthday, but that is not my story to tell. I will, however, say what she always says: that I saved her life that night. I always think that, really, I just saved mine, because I have no concept of how I would live in a world that doesn't include her.

Her sobriety date is my birthday. This past June, I turned thirty-eight years old. She has been sober for twenty-five of them. That following Lent, my grandma gave up drinking. She never picked up a drink again. The following December, my mom married Bill, and they remain married to this day.

Years went by, and in time I met Maggie's dad. We married in September of 2002, and one of the people invited to our wedding was his friend, Pat Haddigan, who lives in Boston. He had actually met Pat at his sister's wedding a few years prior. The two of them fell into conversation, and a friendship began. By all accounts, it was just as simple as that. The kind of friendship that starts with something small, perhaps nothing at all, but forms immediately as if it had only been awaiting the proper order of things.

Every year, Pat flew to Missouri, and they would kick off deer season together at the family farm in Memphis, Missouri—eight hundred acres of property that the Mudd family owns about three hours north of St. Louis. In an effort to repay him for his hospitality over the years, Pat extended an open invitation for us to stay a week at the cottage he and his wife own on Cape Cod in Massachusetts. And in the fall of 2005, for our wedding anniversary, we took him up on his offer.

This was a vacation that I had embarked on with a bit of disinterest, truth be told. By that time, our marriage was falling apart. I could feel it, even if no one else could. We argued, but never really made up. The letters—I still remember the arguments would continue in letters left on the kitchen island. My stomach would sour, and my coffee turned to bile upon finding a letter addressed to me on the counter. These are the wounds that never healed, though I pretended they did. Words are my constant friends, my constant comfort. To see them rise up in attack was a bitter blow, and so I began to keep my words from him.

It was a genuine anxiety of mine that we wouldn't have enough to even talk about if we went on vacation alone, so thank heavens for the presence of the kids. But besides all that, I had become a person who wasn't that interested in vacationing at the ocean. It was an odd thing considering all the fond memories the ocean held for me. Or perhaps, subconsciously, it was because those memories were so precious that I avoided the beach like I did.

Whatever the reason, those past vacations were on the other side of a lifetime ago, and, quite frankly, I had lost track of what had made them so special in the first place.

As we crossed the bridge into Cape Cod, a slight storm was brewing. I rolled down the window . . . and some echo out of the past brought everything back to me. The thunder of the surf that undermined all other sounds. The gritty film of salt and sand perpetually scattered on the kitchen linoleum. I remembered how the beach towels swayed on the deck's railing in air that refused to stand still. And I remembered the evening walks with my dad, and the way the sand was cool—almost cold—on my bare feet.

Little things. Insignificant things. Memories that I could have recalled at any point, yet they went untouched. Unnoticed. Simply because nothing in my present life tapped into them like that first sharp taste of the salty sea air. By the time we pulled into the driveway, I was charged with anticipation. I leapt out of the car into the sea air, and immediately, a heavy wind whipped around me, blowing my hair in every direction at once. It was all the welcome back I needed.

There are times in my life where I think that if I would have never taken that trip, my life would have been easier. And wouldn't have veered so wildly and suddenly off course the way it did. Suddenly, there was a glimpse into the possible future. Suddenly, a memory of a feeling I knew. Suddenly, a shift in my spirit that could not be ignored. And for whatever reason, something unmoored in me on that trip, and I began to drift in an entirely different direction.

By 2007, we were divorced. For a lot of reasons I could go into, but I will not. What would any of them matter now? In the disorienting grief of divorce, I got the role of "crazy." He got the role of beleaguered, brokenhearted, wronged party. To my friends. To my family. To me. To the kids. I can't really explain how so many little episodes got so thoroughly swept under the rug and never became my battle cry for leaving, but they didn't. Because in the darkest, secret chamber of my heart, I wondered if I deserved it. I have always wondered if the main reason for our failure wasn't just that a match was struck in me that burned the whole thing down. I still don't know the answer to that question. As Elizabeth Gilbert writes in her novel Eat, Pray, Love: *"You take all the assets, I'll take all the blame." And that was fine with me.*

Well, no . . . that's not accurate. It wasn't fine. It wasn't even remotely fine. It was just that it wasn't my main focus. Whatever label was applied to me and the ending of our marriage just didn't have the power to horrify me as much as the disaster area that had become my life.

My. Singular.

Me.

My therapist, Judy, remarked to me very early in our acquaintance, "I think you try on lives, and sooner or later they don't fit and you discard them. We need to figure out why you do that." No matter where I looked, I could only see my stats. The stats that made up the story of me:

Unplanned pregnancy

Two kids by two different fathers

Two failed marriages

Thirty-three years old.

I said to her as I sat on her couch one day utterly defeated, "I don't want this. I don't want this to be my story."

She leaned forward and said to me, "Then make a new one."

CHAPTER TWO

2015

"Autobiography in Five Short Chapters"
by Portia Nelson

Chapter Two

I walk down the same street.
There is a deep hole in the sidewalk.
I pretend I don't see it.
I fall in again.
I can't believe I am in this same place.
But it isn't my fault.
It still takes a long time to get out.

8.

roots and . . . roots

When I was a little girl, there was a bank of time when I went to the beach every summer with my dad. He had married a woman named Shelley when I was about ten or so, and every summer, her entire family—all her siblings and her parents—rented a house and took a vacation together. Right there. Right there on the beach. In a house that was bigger, and airier, and breezier than any place I had ever been. It might have been the first time I ever fell in love with an idea, or a life different from my own.

In my mind, it encompassed the whole of my childhood summers, but really it didn't. It was maybe two weeks. Likely one. The houses and beaches varied by year, and I don't believe we ever went to the same one twice. Delaware. Maryland. I have a lingering memory of Virginia, though I couldn't say why. Maybe Rhode Island? And with the exception of one summer—an ill-fated attempt at family camping—I recall my summers on the East Coast with very much happiness and a certain measure of pride.

Sure, I wasn't actually up East the whole time. And truth be told, I didn't want to be. I had a life in Missouri that I liked very much. My summers consisted much more of gymnastics in the backyard of my very best friend Lynn's house, swimming in our pool, sleepovers, running through lazy sunset fields, and working at Klaas', the local market. Then later, as I grew, summer consisted of cheerleading camps, staying up all night with friends, little romances, and working at a pizza place—a teenage rite of passage, if there ever was one.

Eventually, those beachy summers fell by the wayside, and that was okay. It had to be. Dad and Shelley had gone their separate ways, and that way of life reached first its zenith, and then blinked out altogether.

Life rolled along like the tide, and I found myself in my early thirties wondering what my life could look like. What did I want to create for my family, seeing as I was now the head of it? It was up to me alone to determine the direction that our life was going to take, and in the vortex that that kind of was, I could clearly remember those summers—those summers from so long ago. And I used those memories of happiness as a blueprint for the summers I would create for my own children.

Now, for a long time, I only focused on half of it. The coastal half. And I begged, borrowed, and stole to make that be a part of our story. That was a crucial piece of what I wanted for my family, yet it wasn't a piece easily obtained. Some people didn't like it. Truthfully, I didn't like all the parts of it. I am not proud of the person I was in parts of it, but I like where I am now. And that is not a justification—the end does not justify the means—but sometimes all you have is where you land, and you have to find your way back to peace with that.

I once picked up a book at The Brewster Book Store by Anne Lindbergh, who had a particular love for the Cape—which felt kindred to me, especially given her husband had such deep ties to St. Louis. I don't recall much of the book, but I do recall mining it for purpose—*capital P, boldfaced:* **Purpose**—as if this collection of paper and print had the power to make me suddenly aware of what I had lacked the desire or intelligence to see for a few years running. It didn't, of course. It was only a book. In fact, the only thing that struck me at all was her description of types of shells—which, I think you'll agree with me, is rather arbitrary. And yet, encased in the only thing I took away from it was the only thing I needed from it.

She maintained that smaller shells—like youth—are thrown about by the tide. Sharp. All of their life is a reaction to the elements around them. Still others buffet about the sea, becoming more substantial, while at the same time becoming smoother with age. Not as sharp, not as reactionary. Moved about at times by bigger things, but less affected by every ripple of the current. This she likened to the age out of youth but not quite middle age. Still others—oyster shells, I remember!—are the kinds of shells which are essentially immobile. They have attached to things, and like people in middle age, they become both anchored and anchor. Their beauty lies in their constancy. Like a pearl, beauty created through stillness and patience. They strive to be nothing more than what they are because what they are is enough. What they are is exactly what they are supposed to be. They are not thrown about by the sea. They are not the backdrop, for a backdrop can feel irrelevant or ignored. Rather, they are the foundation.

And so—very purposefully—I began to search for the other side of those summers. To value the foundation. Without a foundation, my life is only a reaction to circumstances. A life in which I don't have to know myself. I don't have to choose. I am forever braced *for* change, and *to* change. Yes, that can be a good thing, but it also can be a bit rickety, and not quite dependable or trustworthy.

Judy, my therapist—"Judy the Life-Ruiner" I called her—had a penchant for reaching into the heart of things, the heart of me, and I found her at the time to be . . . well, in a word, *aggravating*, even as we continued as sisters-in-arms along my journey. At any rate, she used to get mad at me because I always said, "I don't know."

I would say, "Judy! It's a good thing! *I don't know* is a person who is willing to try new things!"

She would wave her hand, clearing the air around her of any nonsense.

"Not for you," she would say. "For you, *I don't know* is evasive . . . *I don't know* is the refrain of a person not willing to make up her mind."

I began to notice that the happiness of my summers was on both sides of it, never one without the other. That without side two, side one was untethered. I remembered the home. The deep roots in one place. The swimming pool. The fields behind my house. The streetlights. Little things. The little things which show us that we belong. So, rather than living on a busy street, I moved my children into a neighborhood where they could have friends down the street—just like I did. Because *that*—far above anything else—was my favorite part of childhood.

Soon, I began to remember the feeling I had when I walked into my childhood parish. I could walk into St. Mary's and everyone knew me. So, I began to look for that place for my children, and I found it. When we walk into Assumption Parish on Main Street—we are known.

I remembered the local shops that we frequented when

I was a child. How people took the time to ask about your day. That recreated itself as I began to become a part of our community. The tellers at the bank know us. The people at the local fruit market know us by name—in part because Maggie is so charming, but perhaps it is also because I have a fair bit of it myself. I love that quote by J.M. Barrie: "Charm. It's a sort of bloom on a woman. If you have it, you don't need to have anything else; and if you don't have it, it doesn't much matter what else you have."

Life is an adventure, the greatest one there is. But I have learned over time that you cannot drift. At some point, you need a stopping place, or at least a shelf upon which to rest. A place to go, and people to go to, when you find yourself—as you will—in the eye of one of life's many hurricanes. My life, filled as it was (and still is) with misfires and wrong turns or a run of peaks and triumphs, eventually leveled itself out. Enough that I find myself on the cusp of forty-one, captain of a much steadier ship than I could claim almost a decade ago.

I think now that I have both Massachusetts and Missouri in my life, I notice more than anything the ways in which they are alike. The people: gregarious, thoughtful, in many ways harried and half-crazy . . . but always ready with a hand to help. The stories: all of them winding and filled with so many details that you just have to slow down. Surrender. Offer yourself up to the process of listening. The places: green everywhere, winding roads, hidden treasures off the beaten path. Both places so much more alike than they are different.

I talked to Judy about three months back. Hadn't spoken to her in years. When I began our conversation, I led with, "I'm not sure if you remember me . . ."

She interrupted, "Of course I remember you!"

I said, "Ah. Well. I'm never sure if I'm remembered, and it seems arrogant to assume I am."

She laughed a little. "You, my dear, will have to learn to be a lot less dynamic if you want to be forgotten." Which was so super sweet that I never want to forget it.

We talked a bit. "So, catch me up!" she said, and I did. Near the end of our conversation, she said, "So. Hey. Did you ever make up your mind?"

I asked, "About what?"

"Tell me," she said, "are you a Midwestern farmer's daughter? Or are you a barefoot beachy girl?"

I laughed to remember a time when I tried to paint myself with either one brush or the other. "You know, I eventually *did* make up my mind," I said. "I made up my mind that I am both."

"Yes, of course," she agreed. It was an answer she already knew.

When I found myself at a crossroads about eight years ago, when I put my foot first on this path, I believed truly that I was going to be the one to show my kids the world. Their dad, in my humble opinion, is much more rooted than I am. And I don't mean that in a bad way. In fact, if you asked him, he would be only too happy to tell you how rootless he thinks I am (*Oh, come on! That's funny!*).

But as we stand eight years out, it is he who has shown Maggie more of the world—which I think is hilarious. He has found himself with a woman who likes to travel and—from my perspective—he is starting to get into the spirit of it as well. Which is a good thing. It opens him up a little bit.

By contrast, many people think this thing that I do— summers on the Cape—is a daring adventure, and I suppose in some ways it is. But to me, it is only a second type of home. I travel more *frequently* with the kids, but not more abundantly. The funny thing about life—in fact one of my *favorite things* about it—is its capacity to turn itself upside down, and you with it.

I realized that while I was walking along the beach this morning with my coffee. That the point of life often rearranges itself when you're not paying attention. *Here I stand*, I thought as I looked out at the water, *with my feet in the same sand*. We are in the same place as we have been for the past eight summers. Maggie will go to the same camp again this summer . . . the camp which Will attended once upon a time and then aged out of. As they have grown, they have grown with the same kids. They have grown up under the watchful and loving eyes of the same adults. Our memories are their memories.

We drive the same roads. Look forward to the same ice cream. Play on the same beaches. Here we stand, all these years later . . . different. Grown. Yet the same. And then it hit me.

I did that.

All these years.

All these *years*. Then I laughed to myself.

Who knew? All these years of trying so hard to give my children wings. When all the while, I was giving them roots.

9.

a wish from the sea to me

Houston, we had a problem. The problem was this: *Jakeman*—whose open Wi-Fi network was keeping us tethered to the wide world—was having some technological issues. So, we were at the mercy of some dodgy internet service, as all self-respecting Wi-Fi hijackers do experience from time to time. Did you think I forgot about you? I promise, I didn't. But I did forget about me.

There is something about being here, lost way off to the east of life, that puts me out of touch. I become a bit of a meanderer. But don't let that convince you that I am doing anything particularly divine. I'm not. I'm not doing anything that I don't do at home: reading, laundry, talking to friends, bossing my kids around (from 1,200 miles away), updating statuses. The usual.

And yet . . . not the usual. My sense of urgency is a little bit gone. My days run one into the other. Time goes by with nothing really to show for it. But. *Eh*. Who can say why that really matters anyway? What doesn't get done today will get done tomorrow. As Sam Keen—an American author, professor, and philosopher—once remarked, "Deep summer is when laziness finds respectability."

But all at once, life has delivered me a specific task. Due

tomorrow, in fact. You see, at camp, tomorrow is a special day. This one predetermined and most illustrious day of the camp year, we are charged with presenting a lovely treat to make someone's day. The someone? The name we have pulled out of the hat earlier this week. The price tag? No more than one dollar.

Tonight, my meandering had a specific purpose. I was at Sea Street Beach, on the hunt for a wishing rock. Now, the idea of a wishing rock was a story told to me by my friend Amy years ago. It is a rock, usually black but sometimes green, which has one single band of white running all the way around. A perfect circle. This, my friends, is an excellent gift! A story is free. And a rock is exactly one hundred cents less than a dollar. Genius!

But even better... I love the idea that you can give someone a wish. I had a plan as I walked down the beach. I intended to find this rock on my way out and enjoy the sunset on the way back. So, I kept my head down. I waded in the water. I was very careful to not drop my phone. I was very focused. Looking down so much, in fact, that I was completely surprised to find myself abreast of an entire flock of seagulls. "Oh, hello!" I said when I chanced to look up.

I laughed to myself in that moment. How perfect a metaphor for life I was right then. Ignoring completely the stunning sunset behind me in order to find something. Telling myself I'll enjoy the sunset after I find what I want to find. And it was such a little thing. A rock. But how often do we put off some manner of joy until after we have found what we perceive we need to find?

I turned around. Because what if the sun went behind the cloud and I missed the way it sparkled on the water? No, not in five minutes. Right. Now.

Anne Morrow Lindbergh wrote in her book *A Gift from the Sea,* "The sea does not reward those who are too anxious, too greedy, or too impatient. One should lie empty, open, choiceless as a beach, waiting for a gift from the sea."

Maybe the answer isn't to keep moving, I thought. Maybe the answer is to be still. What if I could trust that this rock would come to me if I would just look up from my furious search and be still for a second.

All at once, it struck me: I do trust that. I utterly and completely trust the universe that much. So I looked up. I took a breath. I felt the breeze. I heard the distant horn of a boat just barely on the wind. I looked at this ridiculously gorgeous sunset. And then I looked back down.

And what should roll toward me? A wishing rock. I laughed. Out loud. Just a spontaneous burst of amusement. Such silly things can be captured by faith. And such grand things as well. But sometimes you pray for big things. Health. Peace. Freedom. Love. And sometimes you just pray for a rock.

I picked up the first wishing rock, then took a step and there came another, rolling in with the tide. Two! I began to walk back, this time enjoying the sunset and everything about it. I found another along that way . . . .and that's life too. Sometimes you find what you're looking for while in motion. Sometimes you have to be still.

It is said that for the wish to come true, you have to give it away. You have to hold the rock. *Wish*. And then throw it back into the sea.

I wondered for just a split second as I glanced back at the water one more time, before stepping onto the road . . . what if someone's wish brought it to me? Maybe God, so steadfast even as I meander and look down, had wished that I would look up. Maybe His wish was that I would notice. And once I did, He tossed His wish into the sea for me.

10.

magic lost

I truly believe that Maggie—at ten—is living out the last of her "believing" years. Believing in Santa Claus. Believing in the Easter Bunny. We haven't seen that Tooth Fairy in a month of Sundays. And if I'm really honest with myself, I have to admit, I outdid myself at Christmas when Maggie made it on the "ANGEL" List and Lucy the Elf came to live with us permanently. Maggie was so profoundly touched by the magic of that—the sheer blessing of it all—that I knew I had done my personal best. Drop the mic. Peace out. *Don't forget to tip your waitress.*

And I think . . .

. . . really, I think I just up and stopped thinking about magical things after that. To the extent that I told a coworker of mine on Friday that Easter has always been celebrated from the religious aspect of it in our family and I "don't even think Maggie ever believed in the Easter Bunny." That's how long gone it was from my mind.

Oh, sure I bought some candy. Bought it, actually, *early* this year. I already had some baskets. But, really. She's *ten,* and I didn't think she believed in the Easter Bunny anyway. Until last night.

Maggie, Will, and I were on the couch watching television, and Maggie said, "Is the Easter Bunny hiding eggs tomorrow morning?"

I, surprised, said, "*Is* he?"

She said, "Yes."

I looked at Will. "*Really?*"

Will said, "Yeah. Every year."

"Every *year*?" I asked him. How could I have completely forgotten about this?

"Yes!" said Maggie.

Crap, I said. But I said that in my head.

Then Maggie said to me, "Mom? Is the Easter Bunny real?"

And I said, ". . ."

We had gone through this at Christmas. Her questions at Christmastime sounded like: "Mom? Is Santa real? Because-I-know-he-is!" She was old enough to ask the question, but still too young to want to know the answer. So this time I waited, judging whether or not she actually wanted to know.

She said, ". . . . . . ?"

I said, ". . . . . . ?"

She said, ". . . . . ."

Then I said, "Come here."

And she said, "No!"

I said, again, "Come here . . ." And she did.

Will, incidentally, had turned as still as a statue, stuck as he was in the middle of this moment. He actually *un*stuck himself long enough to give Maggie's back a rough but quasi-affectionate little rub when she sat down. That—more than anything else—was probably when Maggie really sensed the doom on her horizon.

". . . mmmost of the time," I began, "the Easter Bunny is Mom and Dad."

She didn't cry. Not exactly. But she was quite . . . *ugh*. How would you say it? It was a loss in a way, a little end to the magical innocence of childhood. And it was rotten news to deliver to a girl who just returned home replete with the joy of playing outside all day. A tired little girl who had no idea there was a bit of a ripple in her world lurking just around the corner.

Still. I have to admit, I'm glad Easter opened that door for us and not Christmas. The loss of Santa Claus at Christmastime is a monster kick in the teeth. The Easter Bunny was an easier starting point. After sitting in my arms for about twenty minutes, long after my right leg had lost circulation, she got up.

"I refuse to believe you," she announced, and she went to her room.

Will looked at me with the *"Yikes!"* face, and I made the same face back to him. We sat quietly for a second, then we started talking barely above a whisper.

"When did you stop believing?" I asked him. "I can't remember ever having to tell you."

"I don't know," he admitted. "I don't know if I ever believed, really. I just remember doing the math and thinking . . . there is just no way that actually happens."

I laughed. "I remember, actually, just feeling like I needed to *confirm* with you that you knew Santa didn't exist when you were . . . like . . . twelve. And you said to me, 'Yeah. I know. I mean . . . come on . . . *a sleigh*?'"

We talked for a bit longer. Then Will—who every time I turn around is more of an adult—stopped me when I started to get up. "Just let her be for a while. It's something that's hard to lose. You just have to settle it in your mind alone first." Which made me think there was a time he wanted to believe more than he was willing to admit.

Mom and I talk sometimes at the quiet end of the day. Often Bill is in bed, and so is Maggie. She can usually be found quilting, baby quilt on her lap, in the low light of the lamp by her chair. I carry that picture of her in my mind's eye, and I know I will all my life.

At times like these, I come to her to unburden my heart, and she dispenses advice sometimes—but mostly she just listens while I try to verbalize to her that which I am actually trying to explain to myself. Talking to Mom last night, I was finally able to put into words what I was feeling. The differences I had observed in Maggie and Will as a result of these sweet legends we share with them. And of the eventual loss of them which tears at their hearts a little in the end, and so tears at ours.

I said to her, "Will had a different childhood than Maggie." In many ways, I often think, he was raised by a different mother. So insecure. So young. So unsure of my place in the world. As a result, "Will was more creative than Maggie, but he wasn't as magical. He could pull anything out of the sky and make something out of nothing, but he always knew that what he was creating was fantasy. Maggie believes in magic. Will doesn't." His life was harder. He didn't have the luxury of truly magical things.

I remember one Christmas—long after Will had lost the "Santa magic" of the holiday. We had opened our gifts, the three of us. Maggie, in her innocence, asked what I got for Christmas, and I told her some little something that I have long forgotten. She was practically a baby at the time and was much more wrapped up in her own gifts and the trappings of Christmas morning.

But Will caught the moment and kept it. He looked around. "Did the math" (as he would say) . . . and I watched him realize for the first time that I had no gifts on Christmas morning. That I had spent all my money on them. I *saw* it. I saw the realization drift across his face. If I could choose one moment to take away from him and back into myself, I think it would be that one.

He got up and crossed the room to hug me, and as he did, he said, "Thank you for being Santa to us . . . I just realized there's no Santa for you." Maggie—lost in the new presents and crunching over gift wrap and bows and eating cinnamon sweets—was too young to notice our conversation.

I teared up a bit at the incredible sweetness of him. "But there is!" I said. "All Santa is . . . is *magic*. And you guys are magic to me." He smiled, and I realized that truly, *truly* I had said the right thing. But every year since then, I remembered that look, and I remembered to have a gift under the tree for myself. Where it comes from doesn't matter—I have wrapped up things from my classroom before. It just needs to be there.

This morning, we didn't speak at all of the big Easter Bunny reveal, and I was quite content to follow Maggie's lead. Will was right. The new thought process takes a while to settle in alongside all the rest. Maggie came upstairs. She smiled at her basket. She found the eggs. She shared the contents of her eggs with all of us.

Then she—very deliberately, and filled with much gravity—turned to look at me and said, "Thank you for my Easter basket." And I, with just as much sincerity, replied, "You are very, very welcome."

And in the moment, I was proud of her. Relieved, even, that she seemed to weather this news with grace and without copious amounts of high drama. But, the thing is . . .

Right now. Right now as I'm writing this? I feel a squeeze in my heart.

Because if she doesn't believe . . . then who am I? If I am no longer the bearer—*the creator*—of these fantastical memories with these magical characters, then she and I have lost something. Sure, we've probably gained something else. But it is another step in her journey out of childhood, and even as I show her the way, I wish we never had to leave it. You see, when she believed in magic, I was magic. And I wonder to myself as she grows up a little bit more today: *Without your magic, my dear, where will I get mine?*

11.

carefree highway

Last year, I made the decision to change jobs from the Catholic school across the street to the independent school across the bridge. For those whom I have at a disadvantage: St. Louis is a river town nestled between the Mississippi River to the east and the Missouri River to the west. I, however, live in St. Charles, which was the *first* state capital of Missouri—a little bit of historical trivia you will not be able to escape should you chance to stop by. We will remind you constantly: First Capitol Drive, First State Capital Bank, etc. You won't find the capitol building downtown, but you can have a meeting at the *First* State Capitol Building, nestled along the cobblestone streets directly on the other side of the Missouri River, west of St. Louis.

This decision to make my way out into the wide world, away from my comfort zone of Catholic schools, was made thoughtfully and with an eye toward the needs of my family. The funny thing about making decisions is that there are certain pitfalls or triumphs you become aware of immediately. But then there is this second wave of awareness that looks a lot like grace. It seeps through the ground floor of your awareness, never announcing its presence until it's already there.

When I made this decision, I underestimated the effect that two pieces of this move would have on the overall balance of my life, and I became aware of them both very quickly. First, I underestimated the impact it would have on me to not be in a faith-filled setting. Second, and shamefully much more impactful, I *over*estimated my tolerance for other people and their cars. Bastards. Every one of them.

The first is not surprising. I have been in Catholic schools all of my life. I attended Catholic grade school and high school. I have taught in Catholic schools for ten years. If you're counting, that means that twenty-three of my forty years on this earth have been spent in a Catholic classroom—either in the seats or in the front of the room. So the lack of it was, admittedly, jarring. Ultimately not insurmountable. But certainly a shock to the system.

I missed it. I still miss it. I miss morning prayers. I miss afternoon prayers. I miss all the spontaneous and lovely prayers in between. I admit that a hundred times over, I said these words without thinking about them. But twice as many more times than that, I said them and was completely aware of their grounding effect. The ability of words said in unison to unite a group and set a purpose. Those words—that unity—had the power to ground me to the Here. The Now. While I often forgot to stop and listen to my soul's peace in the presence of those things, I can surely hear the echo of their absence. I miss church bells on my walk back from lunch. I miss crucifixes in classrooms. I miss images of Mary on the wall.

One day, I spoke of this in passing to another teacher. Brief, *brief* conversation. But I think souls have the power to speak to other souls, well beyond our human capacity to communicate. So I think she was not blind to this deep need I had in me, regardless of the length of our conversation. The next day, she walked into my room with holy water. Of all things—it was a little vial her husband had gotten from Rome.

She said, "Don't think I'm crazy—but I'm a holy water fanatic. My daughter always tells me not to flick it on her friends, but I was just thinking last night, and I thought maybe if you could…I don't know…*flick* some in here, or something? Maybe it could clear the energy. Bless it, or something. Maybe it would make you feel like you could make this space a little bit more yours." In that moment, she was the Spirit to me—even in a building not christened Saint Something.

From that moment on, I *went on*. Because that's what you do. You find other joys. You take the hand that wants to help you. You find other ways to ground yourself. You widen your stance and broaden the scope of your balance to include all the peace-filled, faith-filled, joyful, and inspiring people and places in your life. And life does go on.

After a while it's easy. Joy happens everywhere. It's the joke over the salad bar. It's the story out at carpool. It's the new memories made in a new place. It's that kids are kids everywhere and good teachers love kids—regardless of the traditions, or the rituals, or even the lack thereof. Divinity does not have to be acknowledged to exist. And so I find peace where I bring it.

But.

That second thing…

The cars.

There are so *many*.

And I don't mean traffic. Everybody hates traffic…nothing in that is remarkable. Nothing about saying it is revolutionary or unique. No. I just don't like the energy of the highway.

No! Let me not just say *the* highway. Normally I love

highways: the miles of road you can cover, the roadside towns along the way. It's a glimpse of Americana.

Let me whittle it down for you: It's Highway 70, *specifically*. This is the vein that runs through the heart of St. Louis. Through the country, really. When I drive out to the Cape every summer—let me tell you that the feel of Highway 70 is the same in Pennsylvania as it is in Missouri. The jockeying for position. The rat-race feeling.

So, if every morning I turn right out of my neighborhood, I find myself soon on this hellish road, eastbound. Sunshine slowdowns galore. Potholes. There's a curved valley right by Cave Springs Road that, miraculously, makes everyone slow down by a good fifteen miles an hour—as if it's impossible to navigate a vehicle at sixty around a single, mild bend in the road.

It happens again at Zumbehl Road.

And again at Fifth Street. (*Help! There's a bridge!*)

Then we—all of us—get to pause and reflect at the 70/270 interchange about where we are headed this fine morning. South? . . . or North? As if to say, *Hmmm. I drive this every day and still the memory of which lane I need to be in positively escapes me.*

But.

After Easter Sunday—in a little quirky spin on Lent—I gave up Highway 70 and began forty days of taking the back road. The long way around.

You see, if I take a left out of my neighborhood, I veer away from the 70 grind and head on down a quiet back road. Through the north end of O'Fallon, past the tiny tip of a sleepy St. Peters, and onto Highway 370.

Highway 370 has been built for a while—but somehow it just never caught on as a popular travel destination. The road to 370 takes me through windy two-lanes and charming, old, whitewashed barns. Past farmhouses with land spread out in every direction. Cows in their pastures. Irrigation ditches. Large stands of pine trees and dogwoods. On my new morning commute, instead of big rigs and brake lights, I head out of town through farmland, overpasses, and floodplains.

A few years ago, my friend Amy came to visit me from Providence, Rhode Island. We happened to be driving alongside 370, on the outer road, and she kept staring out the window. Back and forth she would look. Beyond her. Behind her. Intermittently, she would push her hand out in front of her as if to test the distance from the road to the horizon—as if she thought it was not real, but rather a painted backdrop that she could touch.

When I asked her what she was doing, she said, "The sky is so big!" She, who had spent some time in the eastern Midwest as a child, said, "I forgot how vast the Midwest can be . . ."

Predictably, I pointed out, "*You live by the ocean.*" She said, "Yes. And if you are near water, you can see far, but most of New England is very woodsy and squeezed together. It's entirely different to see this much room! So much land in your uninterrupted line of sight."

I loved her vision of my home, so I kept it close to my heart—for a lot of reasons. But I think mostly it was because it was something I forgot to be thankful for and I didn't want to forget again.

These days, I no longer have the principal coming over the loudspeaker in the morning, her sudden vocal presence the impetus to make thirty sleepy students rise to their feet. I no longer get to stand with them as we, together, say the Morning Offering prayer. I no longer have days filled with church bells, and Friday morning Mass, and Monday afternoon prayer services. I still love those things. And I still hope to have them back one day. But until then, I no longer have God at His most traditional.

And yet.

He's in the wink of the sun rising over a black, steel railroad bridge. He's in the high, lonesome sound of an early morning train that briefly races parallel to my car before the road curves south. He's in the bend of the Missouri River before it turns the corner. In the farmhouse with the cows in the pasture. The quiet of the morning. The peace of my new drive. And believe me when I say that springtime in Missouri, with the dogwoods in bloom, the fog on the fields—washed in those hazy pastel blues, pinks, and yellows of early morning—is every bit as much God as a prayer in a classroom.

Eventually, 370 drops me off at 270 South, which I don't hate and I do have to travel. I have made a deal with myself over these forty days, that when I get to 270, *then* I can think about work. But while I'm on that carefree, broad back road, I am allowed only to enjoy the sight of the day.

At day's end, I do the reverse. I allow myself to think about work only while on 270. I deconstruct lesson plans. I process my day at work. I talk to myself about what I need to remember for the next day.

But, then. Once I curve through that underpass and come out over the floodplains and farms that spread over either side of 370, I leave it all behind. Right there. Right there on the St. Louis side of the river, I put down my day. I soak in the view that I have chosen.

And I come home.

12.

springtime & bare feet

Spring.
Is.
Winning!

I say that because there is still a power struggle between winter and spring right now in Missouri. But for the most part, spring is WINNING! The sun is up as early as I am. The big, wide-open sky is blue and sunny on the way to work. The rich earth has been turned over. The tractors are in the fields. The sidewalks are filled to the brim with the high school track-and-field team running down Main Street. The thump, thump of the basketball game in the subdivision court, the football game in the gully across from the ball field. These, my friends, are the sights of spring in my sweet, sweet corner of the world.

And though there is so very much to love about this time of year when the whole wide world shakes off the winter blues and renews itself, I have to say that my favorite part of spring...

... is the shoes.

But, wait!

It's not for the reason you may imagine. It's not the color or the style of the shoes. It is the pure and charming *convenience* of them. Spring tips off "leave your shoes in the car" season. "Drive around barefoot" season. "Get your bare feet on the clutch and the gas pedal" season.

I'm not even sure it's legal to drive barefoot, actually. About seven years ago, I recall vividly driving out to Nauset Beach with my friend, Amy. On the way, we had to trade her car for her dad's pickup truck so we could drive on the sand on the outer parts of the beach. The rules for this undertaking were very specific, and I read them in the car. Aloud. To Amy . . . though I believe she'd read them before. Among them, in part:

You have to yield to traffic coming off the beach—even if that means you have to guide the nose of your car into the brush on the side of the road. Well, the side of the path, really. Calling it a "road" would be unnecessarily generous. Additionally, you have to let some air out of your tires in order to not tear up the National Seashore, I suppose. And last, but certainly not least, you cannot drive barefoot on the way there. We cracked up at that. It was a rule so clearly doomed to fail. We were driving to and from a *beach*, people!

So maybe it was that long-ago summer afternoon, with the fresh and lively scented mix of salt and greenery in the air, that made a memory a million miles away from all my other memories. Maybe it was driving barefoot (Yes! Barefoot!) with Maggie in the middle and Amy navigating that great big hog of a steering wheel down a bumpy beach road that imprinted onto my mind a forever-snapshot of happiness. Or maybe I just like to feel the sand under my feet.

I don't quite know why, but being barefoot is the definition of innocent luxury to me. It brings me a sweet little jolt of happiness right where I am. Maybe it brings me back to the girl in me who loved bare feet on bicycle pedals. Maybe it's the woman in me who loved—just this morning—running through a sunrise rainstorm, high heels in one hand, bare feet splashing in the grass. Laughing to myself, as I slammed the car door and threw my heels on the passenger floorboard, at how soaked my clothes got along the way.

But for whatever reason, bare feet in the grass (or in the sand, or on the sidewalk) attaches itself to all my simplest, my most primitive, and my purest memories of happiness. Springtime is my beloved because it brings that all around to me again.

Springtime, in fact, is a woman in bare feet. A little undefined. A little not sure about what's next. A little looking forward, a little looking back. A little bit innocent. And a little bit pagan.

13.

a sort of homecoming

I have often heard it said that when you see people with younger children, the nature of their soul shines through. And as this pertains to classroom teachers, I think—by and large— what you can see of the souls of teachers is often more evident if you are looking at a teacher of the younger grades. How can you not look nurturing when you are so very needed? When you zip up coats for a living, or wipe off tears? How can you not be a second mom to a young one while you hold their hand or patch up a fall?

I wouldn't necessarily say that teachers in the older grades do not have a soul shining through. It is simply a nature that is not quite as evident. As a teacher who has taught from preschool all the way up through eighth grade, I can say definitively that the needs are different. The younger children need a leader. A centerpiece, if you will. The older kids need a follower, of sorts. A monitor-er. Not a centerpiece anymore, but a guiding force to inject balance into a world which—for them—has gone off-kilter.

When I taught the younger grades, my absence from the classroom was met with a glorious sort of horror. *What will we do without you?* The panic! *Have you told the sub who the line leader is? Who will pass out the papers?!* My return during these bygone years was no less glorious than a soldier home from war.

Oh, the hugs! The stories! The love that runneth over. Oh my goodness. There is not a soul who should live and die without the experience of all that warm, strawberry shampoo-scented, syrupy-sticky, lovely affection. It is a love that sees no fault. A love that has no memory of crabby mornings or a sharp comment. A love that has no boundaries. This is the love that is awarded to teachers of small children.

But.

Fifth grade is a different beast. I have often remarked that there is no difference between the amount of love children require. The only difference between teaching younger children and teaching older children is that older children have stopped asking for it. And even if they did ask for it, it is simply not okay to indulge a first-grade style of affection in a fifth-grade classroom. It is hardly appropriate that our love be boundless, or that we be as affectionate with each other as puppies. No, of course not. That would be absurd. But they still need to be loved. And so I love them. Of course I do. How could I do anything less?

I admit to a little bit of a free fall every time I make the switch from the younger grades to older. You see, I am an affectionate creature. I'm a natural hugger. I feel irritated with myself every time I hug someone upon our second meeting. Or, God forbid, our first. It's not a full-bodied hug, but I'm a squeezer. A "hello" side-hugger. My aunt Lou used to say that I was the first one in our family to say "I love you" out loud . . . and I don't know why, but I love people. I adore so many of them. I enjoy a hello. I get a charge out of a familiar face. I am forever walking away from people saying, "Love you!" But, why? *Do* I love them? Sure. I guess I do—it certainly comes out of me a bit unbidden. So the free fall of higher grades, for me, is that I miss the love. I miss the affection. And I don't have it anymore.

This week, I left my fifth graders to go on a camping trip to Onondaga Cave State Park with the fourth grade. This was an experience that my fifth graders (as fourth graders) deplored. It rained. They slept in tents that leaked. They fell asleep wet and woke up soggy and cold. They have relived their horror about this all year, and I have listened. When it was my turn to go, they predicted certain doom.

"Are you staying in tents?" they asked at lunch one day.

"No, we're staying in—"

"*No, no, no, no, no, no!*" I was interrupted. "Do not even *finish* this sentence until it ends in the word 'tents.'"

"—cabins." I finished. And they were livid! Well, *fake*-livid. Fifth graders are not capable of genuine anger. They continued to tease me all last week that I was going to "make meaningful moments with my new class."

"You're forgetting about us already!" cried one of them, all over-the-top drama.

I told them they had a sub, and they only asked who it was. No concern about if this sub would do things my way. No worry about their lot in life without my presence or my smiling face. I told them the name of the sub, and all they said was a unanimous *"YES!"*

No sad faces. No missing me when I was gone.

Then, after two days gone, I returned. While I sat out in the Great Hall talking to another teacher, one of my students on milk carton duty walked by, and for a moment, there was a hitch in his step. Then he said, "Hey."

A few minutes later, another student came out of the bathroom. When I said hello to him, he started to give out a random and vague hello. But when he saw it was me talking to him, he smiled his sweet, little smile, then ducked into the classroom.

I walked by my window on the way to the Specialty Wing, and another student saw me through the window. I gave him the peace sign, and he gave it back. "*Ms. Mudd's back!*" I heard his announcement muffled behind the closed classroom door.

No hugs. No big greeting. But a "hey." A smile. A peace sign.

As soon as I opened my classroom door, one of my girls—who isn't precisely shy, but doesn't know how to say she needs anything—met me at the threshold and said, without preamble, "Oh, Ms. Mudd, I finally heard that new 'Budapest' song you keep trying to tell us about."

"Did you?!" I said.

"Yes! I really liked it."

One of my more voiceless students came up to me just then to show me his completed weaving project. Put it right in front of my face, he did. I told him it was lovely. Because it was. I asked questions about it, and a few other boys explained how they did theirs. All of them talking at once.

"Ooh! I forgot!" I said. "I took pictures!" And they crowded around me to see them. They teased me about my love of "not camping" and asked me my favorite and least favorite parts of my trip.

When they left for the day, they just said goodbye. Barely even that. No hugs. No affection. No "We're glad you're back." But I know something they don't know: just as they need love but don't ask for it, so do they feel love, but not show it.

14.

for my girl

Yesterday evening...

Maggie: "You have to face your fears, Mom."
Me: "No. I don't, actually."
Maggie: "I'm going to bring my friend over and have her wiggle her tooth back and forth."
Me: "Stopstopstop... gross! I won't watch it."
Mag: "I'll clothespin your eyes open."
Me: "I'll poke my eyes out... I don't even care."
Mag: "Then I'll make you listen to it instead! It makes a weird sound anyway."
Me: "Like a popping sound? Like an air pocket? Or a spit pocket?"
Mag: "Ewwwww! Spit pocket?! Oh, sure, loose teeth gross you out—but saying "spit pocket" doesn't."

Maggie Mudd is a lovey girl. She's a plop-down-on-the-couch-next-to-me-and-talk sloucher. She's a lay-her-head-on-my-chest snuggler. She's a disregard-the-book-I'm-reading, lay-her-head-in-my-lap interrupter. A wrap-her-arms-around-me-just-because-she-loves-to-love cuddler.

I am an advice giver. A sneak-a-life-lesson-into-every-moment mother. I'm a crawl-on- the-couch-and-enjoy-this-girl listener. I'm the lap she drapes her legs over. The heart she likes to lean on. The ear she likes to bend. The appreciator-of-the-ridiculous giggler.

> *Mag: "Mom! We should get a lizard! Look at him!"*
> *Me: "We are not getting a lizard."*
> *Mag: "Look at him! He's bright green and has jazzy hands!"*
> *Me: "That lizard would keep the other animals up all night telling jokes."*
> *Mag: "'Hey, everybody! Thanks for coming out tonight...'"*
> *Me: "'A rabbit, a hamster, and a kitten walk into a bar...'"*
> *Mag: "Or he would do impressions of them."*
> *Me: "I guarantee you that somewhere under one of those rocks he has a top hat and a martini."*

And no matter how many random and ordinary conversations we have. No matter how many times we spend a Sunday morning, heads on the pillow, facing each other and talking about cats, *The Avengers*, loose teeth, and new shoes. No matter how many nonsensical conversations we have in the car on the way home from school. No matter how many words ceaselessly flow around me while we talk on opposite sides of the Kohl's dressing room door. And no matter how many conversations we have from opposite sides of the shower curtain . . . I can never get enough. Never get enough of being a mother to a daughter.

Now, don't imagine a comparison. A mother does not mention she loves one because she loves the other less. There is a joy in sons, never let it be said that there isn't. And, oh my goodness, it contains a boundless love! It is an I-will-make-a-choice-between-Marvel-and-DC type of love. It is a love of sound effects, and action figures, and sweaty bangs, and hidden socks, and tripping over Legos at midnight. It is a throw-yourself-on-the-ground love. A roll-in-the-dirt love. A sunny, funny, baffling kind of joy that never, never, never ends. But it is, in many ways, a love that is about letting go.

My Grandma Belgeri was fond of saying, "A son is a son until he takes a wife. A daughter's a daughter the rest of her life." So the love for a son is also a little bit of an I-will-always-love-you-but-not-get-to-keep-you kind of love. A one-day-you-will-marry-someone kind of love, a you-will-not-need-me-as-much kind of love. The love for daughters and the love for sons carry a different flavor. As a mother, you have a different job to do with and for each.

Will will get his faith in women from me. So I will be loyal, and kind, and fair. I will treat him the way I want the women in his life to treat him. But Maggie will get her faith in herself from me. I am her map. Her blueprint for how to treat herself. Her example of confidence. I am the voice in both of their heads, and I better be a good one.

There is a kinship in the love of mother to daughter with a certain us-against-the-world flavor. It has looser lines, holds a freedom of movement. A feeling that I will never have to let her go in quite the same way. Oh, she will break my heart in a million ways, to be sure, but not in that way.

There is a careless intimacy between my Magsie and me that is a balm to my sometimes fractured little soul. Many times we find ourselves stretched out, shoulder to shoulder, on a crooked little couch at the end of a very long day, and I think to myself:

what a thing of beauty she is. What a lovely world she brings to me. And in a tiny, hidden part of me, I count myself luckier than most for a couple of reasons. One, because every mother should have a daughter. And two, because of all the daughters in the world, I get to be blessed with the best one: mine.

15.

the end of in between

There is a ritual that Mom and I have indulged for years now that is forever peaceful. Always fresh. Always a joy.

It is a springtime ritual that takes us from the dinner table, coffee cups in hand, to take a walk out to see her flower garden. There is a sunshine that hits her flower garden *just so* in the late afternoon that sets the whole thing aglow. There is a peace captured there. It's as if the countless hours Mom has spent tending her garden is somehow captured in the air around it. The conversations we've had while visiting it. The encouragement, the laughter, the harmony—all of it has soaked into the roots of the garden, and it holds us in its serenity whenever we chance to visit.

Normally after we visit the garden, we make our way to the back patio and take a seat. The neighbors, Rob and Sarah, are frequently out on their back patio as well, and we exchange some late afternoon pleasantries. It is a constant, this ritual, and last evening was no different.

As we made our way from garden to patio, Mom said to me, "This has been a good time, right? This past year with you living here? It has worked out, hasn't it?"

Before I go any further, let me say that Mom was right. *Yes.* It has been good. *Yes.* It has worked out. Here we stand four short weeks away from moving out of Mom's and resuming life as we once knew it, and *yes*, it has worked out. Very definitely it has. I see that once again, time has taken on that strange elastic quality it has. It seems like yesterday we moved in. It also seems like we are one hundred years away from where we were.

Our former pastor once told me that the "in-between times" are filled with great spiritual possibility. He said, "During transition, we are a little bit cracked open, so grace can get in there—into that openness in us—and really do a lot of work." Additionally, I have always supposed that the old adage, "The Lord is close to the brokenhearted" is inverted. It is probably more likely that the brokenhearted are close to Him. Certainly, I can think of many times in my life when I have been so far down for varied reasons. But when I look back on them, I clearly see them as the times I was also deepest in my faith. There are no atheists in a foxhole, they say. And 'tis the truth.

This, however, has not been a brokenhearted time for me. But it has been an in-between time. On the heels of Mom's question, what struck me more than anything else was that we are—at long last—at the end of in between.

For those who do not know the story, I took stock of my life last year. I think of it as a highway. Just as you need to change lanes on a highway, but cannot stop in the middle of the road to do it, so did I need to take stock and make decisions while still in motion.

What I could see from my perspective was that in the next phase of our lives, I wanted to be in a neighborhood with more friends for Maggie. When I look back at my childhood, the thing I am most thankful for (And when I say "most thankful,"

I mean by a LONG shot. Nearly to the exclusion of everything else.) was that I lived down the street from my very best friend, Lynn. I am so grateful that my childhood was actually an "our" childhood. In my heart, she is my sister. And I have no memories of childhood that don't include her.

So when looking for houses six years or so ago, one of the things that clinched my choice of the house of Saint Margaret Lane was that Will's best friend, Mason, lived three doors down. I once told Will, "In a lifetime of making decisions related to my children—some good and some not as good—buying that house was one of the best decisions I've ever made."

But as Will and Mason grew, so did the median age in the neighborhood. And—beyond that—I really couldn't see myself in this neighborhood for the next decade or so. So a change was necessary. With Will going off to college, we put our house on the market. When it sold, we moved in with Nana and Papa. So began the "in-between time" for Maggie and me.

Mom always says, "You can do anything for a year," and she's right. And it's not even that our circumstances were rotten . . . Oh no, they were the farthest thing from it. We were fed. Loved. Nurtured and cared for. Either Mom or Bill took Maggie to school every morning—and created many an amusing memory along the way. Meanwhile, I forgot what it was like to ever get mail. Nobody needed me. Nobody wanted my money. I was like a free agent for one whole year.

We made memories on top of memories. Dinners. Christmas. Easter. Rainy evenings. Sunny afternoons. This year, we hit the jackpot of sweet memories and put enough of them in storage to last us all our lives. The truth is, Mom and Bill would give the three of us anything—anything at all—and on a silver platter. We have only to ask.

But it was not in their power to give us the one thing we needed the most—which was to LAND. To be in our own space. That was the one thing which time had to take care of. It was as if, back in August, we linked hands and leapt over a giant chasm. Then somehow while we were airborne . . . time stopped. Or slowed. Finally, we are about to touch down again and time will resume its usual pace once more. Will is coming back in the summer. Chloe, our cat, will live with us. Even our possessions—which I don't take much stock by—will thankfully surround us once more.

But along with all this winding down, I am starting to feel the leading edge of this goodbye. It is bittersweet—but in the best of ways. In the way that everything becomes peaceful and lovely and loaded with meaning and appreciation. In the way that I sometimes come upon Mom doing something ordinary and want to memorize her. In the way I enjoy everything about Bill's sense of humor. In the way I count so many blessings and keep them present in my heart.

You see, the end of our in between is the starting point of theirs. Mom and Bill are retiring and moving to Florida. The lineup of the next few weeks is startling in its intensity.

In two weeks, we will have a garage sale. In three, Mom and Bill's house goes on the market. In four, Mags and I move out. In five, school lets out. In six, Mom and Bill go to Florida to look for a new house and I leave for the Cape.

At the end of June, Will arrives home from college for the summer and Mom and Bill will install him in our new house. While he is settling in here, he will also begin helping Mom and Bill pack to move.

By the time Mags and I return at summer's end, the landscape of our lives will be entirely different. No more

Sunday dinners. No more Mom and Bill appearing at our front door with dinner or to invite us out for ice cream.

Even as I mourn that, they have raised me to not fear change—just as I have endeavored to raise my own children the same. Throughout my life, I have watched Mom and Bill link their own hands and leap as well. The fearlessness of them to envision and leap is one of their greatest qualities. They beautifully balance the duty of life with the living of it.

I think everyone is like this to an extent. Everyone is familiar with duty and consequence. The element of choice and action which make up a life. And eventually, everybody settles down in some form or another. I just think some people are born farther away from their ending than others, so they have a longer journey from start to finish.

My friend Cathy once gave me advice that has held me in good stead ever since. She is a bit of a wanderer herself, though she has settled down quite happily in recent years. At any rate, she said to me once on the eve of one of my transitions, "You have to remember that there will be a moment—and you won't see it coming, so you can't predict it—but it will come. You will be sitting in a strange place, with all your shit in boxes . . . half of them unpacked. You'll be completely overwhelmed, and you *will* start crying. And you will think to yourself, *I have made a terrible, terrible mistake*."

And she was right. She continues to be right. In every change I have experienced, that moment has come and gone. The trick is to let it in. The moment itself doesn't mean you've made a mistake, and it doesn't mean you haven't. That moment is just what it is. A bit of a grieving. And it is going to happen. You only get into trouble if you try to convince yourself that it isn't.

The important thing is to acknowledge the unrest in your spirit. Offer the moments of transition their own space to breathe. If transition is a part of change, and change shares space with grief, then the key to letting them go is to first let them in. I once read a passage in a wonderful book which stated, "Treat grief as you would a guest. Let it in, and then let it leave."

I do not think the answer to all unhappiness is change. But I do not believe that the proof of true happiness is constancy either. I think true happiness is malleable. It bends and challenges and waits and pursues. It is now, it is then. It is. It was. It can be. It stays. It leaves. It travels, and it's portable. It runs ahead of you, and it pushes you from behind.

I don't think that when Mom and Bill look back they will ever have cause to say *I wonder* or *I should have done*. I don't think they will ever have the burden of going quietly into their goodnight. I think they don't fear the in between. They do not fear the leap. And they do not fear the landing. They have passed that on to me, and so I pass it on to my children.

I once knew a woman who would say to guests, upon entering her house, "Excuse the mess, we live here." I have always loved how that can apply to home and family—but also to life as well. The big Life. Capital L, *Life*. Just as that woman used to say it about her home, so I would say it about the act of living, in general.

We are adventurers—the five of us. We are adventurers—*all* of us. So, if you please . . . pardon us. Pardon the waves we make. Pardon us as we change lanes.

Excuse the mess. We *live* here.

"God has made everything beautiful in its time.
He has planted eternity in the human heart."
~ Ecclesiastes 3:11

~ Witness, January 2013

Around the time I began life as a newly single mother for the second time, a strange series of coincidences erupted which resulted in me taking a trip to Cape Cod in Massachusetts on my own. The defining realization for me on this vacation was the return of those memories from those summers so long ago. The connection that broke about a decade ago and, with it, broke my heart. I knew in the deepest part of me that I needed to somehow merge my life in St. Louis with the best version of myself I felt on the coast. Being a teacher, I was lucky to have the summers off, so the idea occurred to me to apply for a job at a summer camp. After the vacation, I did so.

By the following summer, I was offered a job at a New England summer camp in Brewster, Massachusetts, and I accepted. In my mind, the kids would go with me and spend their entire half-summer with me up there. Taking in the air, the fresh, salty bite of it. I thought it would be freedom for us—just for a little while. The sun, the waves, and the release.

When I had landed on the Cape—through a madcap series of events—I had ended up staying with the family who owns and runs the camp. Misa is the director of the camp, and her mother is the executive director. Their entire family descends on Marcia's house during the summer. "The Commune" is what Misa's husband David calls it.

The house is a big rambling house on Little Pleasant Bay that has a never-ending supply of summer people, weekend guests, loud family dinner parties, and quiet, cozy corners. It is—to me—a house filled with peace. A sanctuary for wounded souls. They gave me a home when I needed it most. They gave me the time and space to not know who I was. Although that may sound like a strange contribution, it was more valuable to me than anything I could have dreamed of. And it still is today. They allowed me to be a strange and solitary thing. To be an enigma. To be antisocial. To drift in and out of the room and not say a single thing. Because I needed desperately to not be who I was anymore. To not be entertaining. To not be needed. To be left alone.

When I wasn't working, I spent hours walking on the beach. The fact that such a significant portion of my personal journey took place here—at a house by the sea—led my therapist to remark under arched brows, "Oh my, I guess some people even get to fall apart in style . . ."

That first summer, I considered staying on the Cape. I was even offered a job at St. Francis Preparatory School in Hyannis. It was of significant concern to me that my son was having so many issues in so many areas. He was bullied terribly in school. He was failing his classes and sinking further and further into an unreachable depression.

His therapist was concerned that he would soon begin to internalize the—as she termed it— "extremely critical environment" he existed in, and she couldn't know how that would play itself out, but she felt it wouldn't be good. She had even suggested relocation, which was the impetus behind my leaving in the first place. So Will's situation was heavy on my heart that summer.

However, I also knew of myself that my inability to build and sustain a lasting relationship was in some part, small or large, rooted in the fact that I had a father who lived so far away. Whom I had no real day-to-day relationship with. Had I never been to therapy and remained blissfully unaware of how that and other variables fit into my life and shaped me, there would be forgiveness in that. A certain leeway. It would be tragic that history would surely repeat itself in Maggie, but unforeseen and therefore forgivable. But to be aware of the potential damage to Maggie's heart and future relationships made it unforgivable to ignore what I knew. How could I call myself a good mother in one breath and in the next, turn around and place my burden on Maggie's shoulders? I couldn't.

The choice was a painful one. Which child do I knowingly consign to pain? Because it would be one or the other. Will? Who was dangerously failing in his current circumstances? Or Maggie? Who would be a little bit broken before she even started to grow if I moved her away from her dad?

A friend told me before I left, "The Cape always has something to tell you, and it's never what you think it's going to be." And so it was with a very heavy heart that I realized the Cape had called me closer to her, only to tell me to go home.

CHAPTER THREE

2016

"Autobiography in Five Short Chapters"
by Portia Nelson

Chapter Three

I walk down the same street.
There is a deep hole in the sidewalk.
I see it there.
I still fall . . . it's a habit . . . but,
My eyes are open.
I know where I am.
It is my fault.
I get out immediately.

16.

sweet child of mine

Last night . . .

. . . long after Maggie's swim meet was over,

. . . long after we had gone for ice cream to celebrate a season well swum (swam?),

. . . long after I had tucked myself in bed with a cup of hot water and a sleepy mystery set on the bayou in Louisiana,

. . . and long after Maggie had plopped herself on my bed in all her half-dressed glory and pressed me for all the pertinent details of Nana's visit (*What time does her plane land? What time is our pedicure?*),

I said to her, "Isn't is so grand that Nana is coming to visit tomorrow?" And she smiled the smile a grandchild reserves for a grandparent and agreed.

I said, "Doesn't the idea of Nana coming tomorrow make even everything about today better?"

Oh, certainly it did.

And long after Maggie had climbed up into her loft bed and was drawing (a picture for Nana) by the yellow glow of her loft bed lamp . . .

Will came home.

And long after I tracked the sound of him unlocking the front door,

   . . . and toeing off his shoes,

   . . . and opening the fridge,

   . . . and then the pantry,

I heard him walk upstairs and say to Maggie, "Is Mom still awake?"

In my room, I paused in my reading, so in love with the sound of their interactions. I could almost see Maggie pause, pull her headphone off one ear, and say,

"What?"

"Is Mom still awake?"

"I think so."

And he came in to talk to me as well.

After talk of work and schedules and a quick side trip into the Transformers movie, he asked what I suspected he wanted to know all along.

"When is Nana getting here?"

I said, "Around nine thirty," and Will—

Now, this is what I love about him. Will, even at twenty years old, still has this little boy lip twitch of disappointment that he does. After all this time, it still makes my heart swell and hurt at the same time—remembering bigger disappointments reflected in this small, relatively innocuous one.

"I work at nine," he said. And, seeing his betraying twitch of disappointment, I said,

"We will come see you. I'll bring Nana in for you, since I know she is your favorite person on earth."

And although there aren't enough words in the world for me to list the myriad of favorite things I have about this sweet child of mine, this might be my favorite: That he tries to correct me, but in the end cannot. Even as he loves me, he knows I am right. And so I smile to let him know that it is okay. His love for her is not a detraction from his for me. Love is infinite.

But I am right. We both know it is true. Even in the face of his mother, he cannot lie.

His grandmother—Nana—she is the love of his life.

17.

still waiting

There is a place that I once loved.

And I suppose . . .

Yes, I suppose I still do. It is a love which lacks its former luster, its past zeal. A love with an innocence gone, a love with a heavy heart. There is no particular reason to go into the details. Into the story that no longer matters.

I don't particularly want to talk about it, this love. This overwhelming and sudden lack in my life. It is only a place. In the end, that's all it ever was. Brick and mortar. To imagine that it ever stood for anything more than that is to imagine it wrong.

Plus, I don't like to acknowledge burden. Or the twin forefathers of burden: disappointment and loss. It seems to me that life holds so much hope. There is too much to celebrate to dawdle in disappointment for long. But it is equally true that a grief not acknowledged can't process itself. It stays in the corners of your mind and inside the beats of your heart. It rides along with the synapses firing in your brain. It becomes a silent, secret part of your interactions and thoughts. Just waiting. Waiting, waiting for you to give it room to breathe.

I don't know about you, but I don't care for drawn-out emotion. As my mom will tell you, "Ramona does not care for a martyr," and to a certain extent, that's true. I hate to imagine that I am that hard of a person. Surely I have a bit of softness to call my own, but I do grow tired of a martyr. Especially when the martyr is me.

I can remember a conversation, years and years ago, with my therapist. In this long-ago conversation, Judy was trying to clarify something. We sat in this office, overlooking Lake St. Louis. The sunset was stunning, I'm sure, though I hardly noticed it on evenings like these.

"So, let me get this straight," she said. "You are going to allow a person back into your life who hurt your feelings very much, but you aren't going to require that he explain himself or *apologize*?"

I said, "I disagree with you. I think he apologized in his own way."

"What's wrong with the standard way?" she asked. "Words like 'I'm' and 'sorry'?"

"*Eww!*" I yelled. "It's embarrassing!" The suggestion like nails on a chalkboard to me. "People can keep their emotions to themselves, Judy . . . what the hell am I going to do with them?"

Then she started laughing.

"What? What are you laughing at?"

"I just find it kind of funny . . ."

"What?"

"I find it funny that someone who is so emotional herself can't tolerate other people's emotions."

I pointed at her. "That's not true. When my friends are sad, I am happy to help them."

"I would argue that those aren't your emotions. But," she put up a staying hand, "*but* you are right, that is true that you are a friend to anyone who needs you. Allow me to rephrase: *You don't like to deal with emotions that might accidentally snag your own.* That's when you shut it out. *That's* when you don't want to hear it."

Angry, I shouted, "*That* is *NOT* true!"

She looked at me hard. "Lady, I can hear the door slam."

What happened recently was that this place, this place I have loved, found itself a house divided. Its members at odds. As usual, I expressed my opinion. In response, people expressed theirs. Some opinions were thoughtful and well-expressed. Some weren't.

Opinions ran the gamut from being hot-headed or defensive to supercilious and kind of patronizing. In the end, it doesn't really matter. The fact remains that there is a basic truism of humankind that is always in play. It is that people define what they agree with by its best example and define what they don't agree with by its worst. And until we are willing to put away the armor of that style of communication, then we're never trying to communicate. We're only trying to win. And I am as guilty as anybody else on that front.

In response to this contentious, stunning brokenness, I immediately attempted to shield those who I felt were hurting and was sucker punched by the profound pushback. Emotionally, I was horrified. I think I spent three days crying. For myself. For those I was trying to defend. For those who couldn't see it. For those who couldn't speak, and for those who *wouldn't* speak. Who are you? *Where are you?* It was like I was speaking to people who only understood half of the alphabet, so content were they behind their privilege.

I couldn't comprehend the lack of generosity. I couldn't countenance the absence of basic awareness. And for the first time in my life, I was embarrassed to be considered a member of this place.

And as I am wont to do: I left.

I went into myself. I went into my house. My family. My friends. My lovely, lovely work—which is absolutely a place a gal could lose herself in. I pulled the curtains closed to the outside world. *No, you may not enter. You may not have the pieces of me.*

But.

The sun will come out. And 360 degrees from crazy is still crazy. Eventually, I was called back to this place. I was called back, oddly enough, by a responsibility that I had signed on for. I had promised to . . . host something, shall we say . . . once a week. I found myself back on the grounds for the first time in . . . two months? Six weeks maybe?

I was nervous. Could everybody see that I no longer belonged? That I had separated myself, my heart, from this place? Was my anger being broadcast in great waves of polluted energy, even as I tried to remember that anger had no place in the particular moment I was in?

Was it? I didn't know.

A long time ago, I was talking with some friends. A bunch of us were sitting in Adirondack chairs around a bonfire at a Cape Cod locale we sometimes frequented. It was a summer night. Breezy. You know how it is by the water. Nights are chilly, made even more so by the fact that your skin has been in the sun all day, so even a light breeze kicks up a path of goosebumps in its wake. We were wearing sweatshirts, our toes close to the heat from the flames, chatting. Laughing, from time to time, over little bits of our day.

At some point, the conversation turned, and a friend who was sitting nearest me was teasing me about loving someone.

I can't even remember how this conversation came about, but she felt that I was—unbeknownst to my own self—in love with this person back home. How silly. I said to her, enjoying the moment, "If I am in love with *him*, then love must not be at all what I think it is."

She laughed. "Oh, I imagine that is entirely true ..." she said.

And the thing is, I was right. Romantic as the notion was, she didn't have all the information concerning this long-ago maybe-of-a-man. But the idea stuck with me. That love could be different than I thought it was. Or, more specifically, different than I wanted it to be.

Back then, and perhaps a little bit now on my more wistful days, I wanted love to consume me. To block out everything else. To hold me within its grasp and never, ever, ever let me go. To make decisions easier, burdens lighter, and life happier. And to a certain extent, it does. Love *does* have the power to do all of those things. Love has done those things for me.

But you can also love with a heavy heart, and that was a lesson long in the making for me. That a heavy heart wasn't a lack of love, simply a different face of it.

I don't think one is stronger than the other. It's not a tally or a competition. But I don't think anyone would disagree with me that the love that sees through the heavy heart possesses a gritty endurance that a lighter kind of love lacks. One loves *because*. The other loves *although*.

Still. I am a creature of habit. And even now, I would un-choose this place. I am that disappointed by it. But Maggie loves this place too, and my fight is not hers. So I came back. I came because sometimes love looks like duty. I came because sometimes love looks like doing what you said you were going to do. Sometimes love looks like refusing to let yourself down, and I would let myself down if I allowed my disillusionment to lead me to disappoint others.

I was in a church the other day, and I said to God, "I am angry. *Still.* I'm not asking you to take my anger from me—you probably couldn't even if you wanted to because I'm still holding it too tightly. But I need your help. I would like for you to please help me be a better person than I want to be. At least for the sake of the people who need me to be."

So for now, I am here. And I will faithfully uphold what I am here to uphold. But I can't promise anything beyond that. I am frozen, loving this place *although*. It's all I've got in me.

I don't know where I'll go from here. Sometimes a person wanders around in the Land of I Don't Know for a while. That's okay. I have God holding my hand through this, as much as I keep trying to shake Him off. I think He's amused from time to time, as I have so fully blamed this on Him. What do I think? That He has the power to stop people from disappointing me? Yes, in fact. That is exactly what I think, so we're not on speaking terms.

But my God is a long-suffering God. An eye roller. A Mona's-in-a-really-bad-mood-so-leave-her-alone type of deity, and I have become petulant, really. And do you know what? I'm kind of enjoying it. Forty-two years into life, and I get it. I finally get what Judy was saying.

So, no. People don't get to apologize "in their own way" to me.

I'd like an "I'm" and I'd like a "sorry."

18.

lights out

I have this neighbor.

I can't help it that she's an oddball. I call her Weirdie, and it's the only thing I do that Maggie doesn't entirely care for: that I have a name for this woman. It's not really anything born of malintent, it's just what we do in our family. My mom and stepdad always named our neighbors: The Vampire; No Chin; Trish the Dish; Chuck, Chuck Bo Buck . . . it's just what we do. But besides all that, Maggie likes to imagine that I am only made up of kindness and nowhere in my nature is even a whiff of contrariness. But I can't help it. I really can't remember this woman's name anyway, and she's—as one of my good friends would say—"a bit of an unmade bed."

Case in point: For the past two weeks, she has had her kitchen light on day and night. All. Night. Long.

"Do you think she's been murdered?" Maggie and I say to each other.

"No. I've seen her get in her car and go to work."

The glow of her kitchen light sneaks into my bedroom window, and it's like a full moon every night.

"It's like sleeping on the surface of the sun!" I said to

Maggie as we stood at my window last night, peering at the (not) darkness in the backyard.

"It is not," she said.

"All the baby sea turtles can't find their homes anymore! Ugggh!" I yelled at Weirdie from my window. "*Turn off your light!!*"

"Mom! We live a thousand miles from the ocean. The sea turtles are not . . . oh, nevermind."

I have this mosquito bite. Maybe a spider bite.

It's right on my forearm. I got it at recess yesterday. "Don't look at me, I'm hideous!" I told my class at lunch. It's deforming my arm, and it doesn't respond to "itchy cream"— which is the name that apparently every single person in the state of Missouri, young and old, uses instead of hydrocortisone (myself included).

"Do you have any itchy cream?"

"The office probably has itchy cream."

Everyone from my daughter, to my coworker, to the pharmacist at Walgreens. "Have you put itchy cream on it?" Why, yes. I have.

Last night, after fake-yelling at Weirdie, I decided to take some Benadryl for the swelling of this bite. Benadryl makes me sleepy, so I took the medicine and then went to read in bed.

I have this daughter.

She came into my bedroom last night to find me fast asleep. Book on the floor. Glasses on the pillow.

I surfaced briefly when I felt her kiss my cheek. She pulled up the covers and said, "You look so cozy in here." I tried very, very hard to say, "You can lay down with me," but I think it came out as gibberish, if it came out at all. Truthfully, I worked hard to organize the scraps of thoughts into words, but the rain and the Benadryl kept luring me back to the Land of Nod.

But I remember this daughter of mine. Just before I went back under, she whispered, "*Sweet dreams,*" and walked to the door.

She stopped. Huffed. Honestly, *huffed*. Then crossed over to my window and, with a hand on each curtain, decisively pulled them closed.

Good night, Mama.
Sweet dreams, baby.
Lights out, Weirdie.

19.

the forgotten things

Yesterday, I went to a funeral. The funeral of my stepdad's father. He was ninety. A good, long life. A good man. It was nice to come together as a family. I'm conscious of the little blessings along the way, like seeing Mom and Bill at a time I hadn't anticipated. An afternoon with Maggie I hadn't foreseen. An arm-in-arm walk with Will down a sunny hallway, a quiet moment of connection I hadn't planned.

Today, Maggie turned twelve. Goodness does time march on. Birthdays are such markers of time, and they always make me a little melancholy, only because surely there is something I meant to accomplish, but I didn't. They are proof of our inability to hold time. And funerals are, of course, the same. So I am of two minds on these two days, and have felt contemplative as a result.

I talked to Will, this beautiful son of mine. Just for a bit. He's been a little off himself lately for reasons that are not mine to share. I had the mother's burden of needing to find the correct mix of letting him wander alone and making him reach out for the hand I could see he needed. He is such a love. I remain so proud of him always.

My love for him is such a completely different animal than my love for Maggie that to be in their combined presence, or with each of them individually, is to be in constant awe of the myriad ways a heart can love. It is truly an incredible machine, the heart. It beats outside of my body, vulnerable, at all times on behalf of these two. I can only hope to be able to find a new kind of love again one day. Maybe there is a third kind or a thousandth kind I have yet to feel.

But, I sit here now. The storm outside energizes my spirit. I feel refreshed. I forgot for a while how blessed I was. How blessed I am. I think we all have those times when we forget to be grateful. We forget to remember the bonds which unite us. The spirit that holds us in communion. The things we all share. The moments we connect to humanity. To others. To ourselves, and to the selves we keep protected. We remember that to love someone *because* is wonderful, but to learn to love *although* is an incredible exercise of the spirit.

This world. It moves so fast. It demands such time and force and forward motion. But how about the moments where we slow the momentum? Just recently, and in a world where Maggie is moving so fast, she has—without warning—become enchanted with Scooby-Doo again. The sound of her watching like a beloved echo out of the past. A last-minute grab onto what she forgot to remember. A choice. A choice to not give up delight or whimsy. To choose to keep the simple.

And I have once again become fascinated with the simple as well. The sunshine on the hardwood. A deep, cleansing breath. A morning sunrise stretch. A snoozing cat at my elbow. Rain. Thunder. Warmth. Joy. The bliss that life is when you let it be.

I have been reminded of the ways that life can tilt on its axis and terrify the mind and heart. Now I am on the other side of that and am a better person for it. Hopefully.

Now, at peace, I remember what was forgotten. I look around and pick up the pieces I dropped in my fear. The parts of me I set down in my entitlement. The things I abandoned in the ungrateful moment. I blink, and I remember my blessings. I blink, and I remember a life in progress.

20.

life: a narrative

I feel like I wake up every day wondering: *Do I love my life?* Really. No, seriously. *Do I?*

A coworker of mine said something in passing the other day, and it captivated me. She said, of someone else, "You know how some people have an inner narrative they tell themselves and it is so clearly false that they need someone to hold up a mirror to it?"

We went on. We stood on the ball field and had an entire conversation about this nameless, faceless person whom I've never met and her false narrative. And I was in the conversation—I was. But part of me was also apart from it . . . *scanning . . . processing . . . buffering . . .*

Ohmygod! The thoughts that swirled around me!

Am I like that? What if my narrative is false? What if I'm lying to myself about all I hold dear? What if I actually *do* want a white picket fence? What if I am secretly sad about the state of my life and I'm very skillfully hiding it from myself and passing it off as truth? What if my tears are cried out and my heart is wrung dry . . . a barren oasis in which I refuse to feel or love ever again?? Let me tell you, friends, these are questions that have broken greater women than I.

This random conversation wasn't the beginning of this thought process for me. No, but it gave it a little jump start. Like the paddles on a cardiac arrest victim's chest, I was jolted into a need for self-awareness. Even *more* self-perusal, if you can even imagine. I mean, this was next-level stuff.

Like *Groundhog Day*, I already start over every morning at the beginning. So I don't really need to be thinking even more. A significant portion of my brain is occupied daily with the quest to remember that I don't have to think so hard. That not every sunrise is an existential crisis. The truth is—I do like my life. (I do, right?) Yes, I suppose I do.

I wish I knew how it was all going to turn out. Wish I knew where I'd end up. Wish I was already there. But, oh well. That's life, right? We all ride on without a destination. And I don't want to look back and find out I've lived my life wrong—that's a great fear. But I would probably saddle up that fear given any path I took in life.

If I'd gotten my original dream and settled down with my first love and had a passel of kids . . . I bet I'd still be waking up at forty-two hoping I didn't live my life wrong. Having simply chosen nothing but what was originally presented to me wouldn't have calmed my restless spirit. I know enough about me to know that.

If my first marriage had worked, or my second one . . . I bet I'd still spare a stray moment at forty-two to hope that life was on plan. If it had worked out with this guy, or that guy, or this hadn't happened, or that had . . . I still don't imagine I'd have escaped the fear of a wrong turn. Especially knowing what it's like to live in a searching mind like mine.

Good things came out of all of these experiences, of course. Little Divine things. Things I did nothing really to deserve, but will do everything to keep safe and whole. Will, of course. Maggie. Such Divine blessings. There are no words for the richness they give my life. The purpose. The care of them defines me in every single way there is. I am blessed with them, by them, and because of them. My contentment with the life I've given them, and my pride in it, is endless.

Yet. Some mornings—all mornings—I have a moment to wake up and wonder. *Am I doing this right?* Some days I wake up and wish I lived anywhere but here. Maine, Dallas, Burlington, Vermont. Cape Cod. *Why* did I never settle on Cape Cod? Wait, no . . . I do know why. But, Providence! Michigan! *Anywhere*. Hell, even St. Louis itself rather than the suburbs.

But, the truth is, I'm doing exactly what I should be doing right now. Even my endless projections can forecast that much. I can't see the future, no, and I can't see around the bend of the side roads I didn't turn down. But I can see the present clearly enough, and I know this: it steals my heart every single day.

School mornings, for instance. Bliss! Maggie's alarm beeping in the dark, letting me know it's time to stop staring out the window and start getting ready for work. Her, freshly awake, warm and sleepy, shuffling in wherever I am. A hug that lasts a bit too long and is suspiciously heavy—like, perhaps, she might have blinked herself back to sleep on my shoulder.

The times Will walks back through our door to surprise us with his collegiate presence at dinner on a random Thursday (and to not-so-much surprise us with laundry as well). Sitting in his (now) normally empty chair, telling stories from the week. His darling unshaven face. Keys on the counter. Perfectly content to forgo a plate in favor of eating the rest of the dinner on the table straight from their serving bowls.

There is so much feeling squashed into my life that I can't imagine being more blessed. There isn't more contentment even *possible* for me. And I would know . . . I've looked for it! These trees that dance around out my window every morning. I love them! Their holy breeze. Friends and books and a good job and familiar streets and dreams and accomplishments and plans and people who make me laugh . . . and, yes, even random conversations that happen on a soccer field that send me into a spirally free-for-all. Even those I love—because I love the clarity they ultimately produce.

Fall is coming, gorgeous fall. And life is so good that I feel like I'm cheating on a test. Is it wrong that I am so content that I wouldn't even consider adding anything else to my life?

Is it? That I don't know. That I wonder.

Mags and I were in the nutrition store the other day, and I was positively jazzed about the way the lavender oil I had just bought fit into one of the sweet little pockets in the purse my mom had made me. Then, to make the moment even more amusing to the clerk, Maggie came over and gushed over the same exact thing.

"Oh! Look how it fits just right in that pocket!"

The clerk said, "Well, it's the little things in life."

Maggie said, "Yes, it is!"

I smiled at her and said, "Well, there aren't enough big things to make you happy enough often enough . . . so it'd better be the small things that do the trick!"

The sales lady loved that, and honestly, so did I. I often say things I haven't thought of yet, and I love when it happens and I manage to look inspirational rather than ridiculous and socially awkward.

The thing is.

The thing is, every morning I wake up and wonder. I admit it, I do. You may find that irritating. I once had a friend roll her eyes and yell, "JUST LET IT GO!"

But I can't. I don't. I won't.

I won't believe that I can't still send out forgiveness to those whose lives no longer cross mine, or send out the *I'm sorry* that I'm too afraid to say. And it's not a holding, like a burden. But a holding, like a keeping. I want to keep well the hearts, or parts of hearts, that have been entrusted to me. And I want to hold well my own. I want to make sure that—like *Groundhog Day*—I do better than the day before.

Every morning, my life arrives in fits and starts. Stages of clarity that I can sometimes capture and sometimes not. The landscape twitches and shifts depending upon my mood, or the amount of sleep I got, or the moon. But in the end—at the end of a life, or a year, or a summer, or a day—or at the beginning of it, it's just a life lived. No more. No less.

Did I miss something along the way? The answer is probably yes. *Of course.* We all did.

But then I sneak into this private morning time. I move a sleepy cat off my feet at the foot of the bed. I look out my bedroom window, out at the dark dawn. I see the flittering of moonlit, silver leaves on trees, fresh from an overnight rainstorm, released from their branches by the winds of fall. It energizes my spirit, this soggy, early morning. The rain has coaxed so many leaves to the ground. Released from their moorings, these leaves skip away on the early breeze, and I remember that a life is no less rich for having learned to let go.

The dawn comes, the sun glows from under a bruised overnight cloud, and I am aware that I have always known the answer. Peace settles into all the parts of me.

Yes. Oh, yes, of course I do. What's not to love?

All life is, is a story, and all your happiness depends upon loving your narration of it. On the flip side, all the shades of misery can be found in believing someone else's narrative of your life. The stories other people tell you about you. Or worse, the sucker's bet of comparing narratives. That's a trap if there ever was one. The idea that your life narrative and mine should be going in the same direction or be in the same place on equal journeys is so very distressing. They're not. They can never hope to be. They're not *supposed* to be.

And unless your narrative is keeping you in a place that is unhealthy or abusive in some way, then go with it. Who cares? Of all the narratives the world will provide for your life, and the good Lord knows there's no shortage of them, I sincerely hope you choose your own. No one knows your story like you do.

I frequently tell people who are facing a nerve-wracking situation, "In eight hours, this will just be a story. So make it a good one."

And so I say the same to you. At the end of this day, at the end of this week, at the end of this life . . . this will only be a story. Be good to yourself. Tell yourself a good one.

"What man of you, having one hundred sheep, if he lost one of
them does not leave the other ninety-nine in the wilderness,
and go after the one which was lost until he finds it?"
~ Luke 15:3-4

~ Witness, January 2013

My first summer on the Cape, I met John. John was a bartender at a little Irish pub in town, and he and I got along very well. I went back to St. Louis in August, but I came back to visit him in November. I met him at the pub. He was working and very excited to see me and introduce me to his friends. I stayed until closing time, and we talked until about 2 A.M. Eventually, we ended up in my hotel room.

At around 4 A.M., I woke to a banging at the door. "I know who that is . . ." he said. I assure you I did not. It didn't take a genius to figure out what kind of hot water I had landed in, though. He tried to get me to open the door and tell her that I had no idea who he was, that she had the wrong room. But I was wary of a bunch of yelling and crying happening outside a closed door and refused. Had that situation been visited upon me today, I would have opened the door and thrown him out, but I was in a different place back then and couldn't really process any of it.

I had children. I was a Catholic school teacher. How had my life come to this? A dingy hotel room. A woman banging on a door that I couldn't open and a half-naked man, who had forgotten *all about me, trying to climb out the window. I got up and took a shower. Eventually the banging stopped. He went home.*

The next morning, I woke up mentally gritty and exhausted from my evening. I had thought that John and I were going to spend the entire long weekend together, but it was obvious that wasn't the case. I called Marcia. I announced my impromptu arrival on the Cape as if I was just so flighty that it just slipped my mind to let her know sooner and . . . by the way . . . could I stay there the rest of my trip?

From my thirty-four-year-old perspective, I thought I had sold it rather well, but a woman of sixty-seven who was already one of the wisest women I'd ever known couldn't have missed the air of disaster surrounding my arrival. She said to me in the middle of my explanation, "Honey. You're here. That's the part that matters. I am on my way out the door to a Rotary meeting. But there is food, there is a fire in the woodstove, and I just want you to come home." And so I did.

The house in winter is a bit of a sleeping giant—absent as it is of the people and energy of summer—but I needed that. An empty house. I went up to my room and slept for hours. When I awoke, the sun was setting. Downstairs, I made a cup of tea, then grabbed a sweater out of the kitchen closet. The path to the beach is well-worn, the crunch of gravel beneath my feet a comfort I hadn't known I needed. There is a rock that stands about halfway down the beach about as tall as my waist. It's big and heavy and has the most uncomfortable barnacles on it, but it's there. A bit like The Giving Tree. Giving me support and a place to lean and not feel like such a failure all the time.

That night, I woke up in the dead of night to my name. Just my name. Truly. I went from REM sleep to fully alert in a single moment. "Mona!" I sat up. I saw nothing but the glow from the kitchen skylights a floor below me. I returned to sleep on a perfect moment of grace. The feeling didn't last forever. But it was there, in that moment. I am here, it seemed to say. I am here.

By my second summer on the Cape, John had talked his way back into my life, and regardless of the earlier revelations, I welcomed him. I forgave him. Why? I don't know . . . I guess I just wanted one thing to go from bad to good instead of bad to worse. We had communicated all winter and spring, and I was desperately excited to see him again. We planned for me to travel up to New Hampshire—where he lived by then—on my first weekend on the Cape. He gave me his address. I packed an overnight bag and began my three-hour drive north. I spoke to him when I was in Boston—I was held up a bit by traffic and the rain.

When I finally arrived at the address he had given, it was a nursing home. Not a house at all, and certainly not his house. I called. He never answered. I sat in the local church parking lot for a while. Around midnight, I drove back to the Cape. I arrived at the house around 3 A.M. I had to wake Marcia up to unlatch the screen. I went in and went to sleep.

I never spoke much about it to anyone. Although I will say that the following morning, directly after pouring her coffee, Marcia said to me—requiring neither an intro nor a response, "You know. I just don't think that being in love means you have to be emotionally terrified all the time."

I began to find little ways to digest this. I had never before encountered a soul so very unkind. I had some struggles in life, sure. But for the most part, I had always been loved. Cared for. To meet someone on the road who saw me as only shrapnel, willing to sacrifice me as collateral damage in the desolate life he led, was shocking. Intellectually, I understood it. But to my psyche, it was completely foreign, so it took a while. To be nothing at all to someone. Nothing but what? A joke? A bit of sport? To be cared for so little. It leaves a mark.

I think I kept trying to find ways to make it matter. To make it not such a stupendous loss of precious time. I kept searching for that final text. That final phone call. That final concluding sentence that would make sense of it. That would allow me to close the door. And he wouldn't give it to me. He was just gone. A cliffhanger without a season premiere.

I never heard from him except for one time months later, possibly a year. I was home by then, back in Missouri. Moving into my parents' house while we were preparing to build a new one. The chime of the text was lost in the activity of the day, but when I looked at my phone, I was surprised to see a text from a New Hampshire area code.

"I miss you."

It took me a second to process the type of ego that would imagine that this was a welcome intrusion after so much silence. But I'm no stranger to ego, no stranger to wrong turns. But how to respond? Do I respond out of anger? Spite? Do I respond with silence? But no, that isn't me. I took my time. "Speak in haste, repent at leisure," as my mom often quotes.

I picked out the letters and began to type.

"You know . . ." I typed slowly and with a gravity of how heavy this was to me. No longer hurtful, and I was not a perfect soul either. My desperation at that time in my life, to hold, to keep, to avoid, was embarrassing to remember. It made me a version of myself I didn't like to think about. I deleted the letters, then started typing them again.

"You know what? I'm going to need for you to keep this door closed."

As a nod to whatever scraps of honor a man like that, living a life like his, can claim—he did just that. He did not respond. And I never heard from him again.

CHAPTER FOUR

2017

"Autobiography in Five Short Chapters"
by Portia Nelson

Chapter Four

I walk down the same street.
There is a deep hole in the sidewalk.
I walk around it.

21.

a universe of difference

I don't have Maggie this week. More often than not, when I find myself without her, I scrape the bottom of the barrel of things to do. Not that I am avoiding her absence as much as I am embracing the things I usually eschew in her presence: the bottom of the To-Do List things, the boring things, the solitary Must-Do's. Today, I was rooting through boxes. Rooting through time, as it turned out to be. Going through a few plastic bins, just positive that I could clear them of their junk and free up one or two for other household uses. There, in the bottom of the bottom bin, I found a green duffel bag, "*Newport*" emblazoned on it in a white, old-fashioned font. *"Alive with Pleasure!"*

I laughed. This was a bag given to me by my friend Lynn on the occasion of my fortieth birthday. "I couldn't WAIT to give it to you!" I remembered her saying at the rainy winery almost three years ago. "I found it in my mom's basement!"

Newport—in case you are not aware—is a brand of cigarettes that debuted somewhere in the early '80s. I'm not sure if it debuted in America or if it simply debuted in our lives, but either way, there it was. Lynn's mom was a sales rep (or something) for Newport. I'm not sure what she actually did for the company, but I am positively sure she did it only to get free cigarettes. So there we were, a couple of ten-year-olds, *Alive with Pleasure!* The tagline decorated our (new! free!) t-shirts. It was on our duffel bags, on our plastic cups of Tang, on Lynn's mom's cigarette lighters. *Newport!* The word zipped across whatever item it graced—an inverted Nike swoosh before Nike was cool. *Alive with Pleasure!*

Lynn and I, somehow, even at barely ten years of age, were clever enough to add an irreverent addendum after their catchy slogan. *"Newport: Alive with Pleasure!"* proclaimed our new wrist sweatbands, and we would look at each other and whisper, "... but not for very long."

Inside the duffel bag was a white paper bag filled with letters written to me by friends when I was on a spiritual retreat a few years ago. By the light of a single bare bulb on one side of the basement, I reread them. Sitting on an old, dusty, plastic box, the hum of the air conditioner fell away, the arms of the clock circled on without my noticing. Some notes were short, some long. Some made me cry, and some made me laugh. Some I remembered, some I had forgotten. Piles and piles of letters and cards. These, the messages which greeted me from around the country on my last retreat day. One was from a friend I have known since the summer before high school. She wrote:

> "First, know that I feel immense pressure writing to you
> as I do not have your gift of words and missed the day
> in school when they explained split infinitives. But . . . I
> feel like we are always on the same page, even if you are
> able to verbalize that page much better than I . . . Life

may take you all over the country, but no matter where you go . . . you are always you. Thank you for your gift of friendship. Thank you for the risks you take in the name of love. Thank you for your inspiring words and stories. Your gift of laughter is priceless."

I returned the letters to their place and could see that resting inside the white paper bag where I had found the letters was a journal. Of all things! It made me smile to see one from so long ago. I must have at some point thought it worth keeping because it had the distinction of being not only intact, but labeled: *2012 – Cape Cod Summer.*

Inside was a smorgasbord. Pictures with glitter made by Maggie, postcards, notes that greeted me on summer mornings, drafted in red marker: *"THANK YOU for everything you do, Monamudd. You are a treasure!"* The message written inside a heart and taped to my desktop screen. A handwritten note placed on top of my suitcase the night before I left for home, *"Mona-Dear, today and always please remember the abundant love which surrounds you—"*

A card taped between two pages, whose signature page proclaimed from a friend, "I'll keep an eye on you this summer, but then again . . . I'm not very responsible."

Tickets to the Monomoy Theatre in Chatham to see *Henry IV.* Playbills. Drawings. Journal entries. Lists. Miscellaneous numbers added and subtracted equaling something that answered a once-upon-a-moment's question. I delighted to discover "Monamudd's Criteria for a Mate"—which was a little thirty-point list that Misa and I had crafted one stormy summer night over tea. God what a storm that was! I had forgotten until now how a storm can rage by the sea. I noticed the date on the list: July 24, 2010. I must have lifted that from some other journal and stuck it in this one to keep.

Random quotes were scattered about this journal, some of them lofty—*"For I have learned to be content whatever the circumstances"* ~ *Philippians 4:11*—and some of them not. Written on the sides of pages, horizontal and vertical. In the upper margin, or squeezed into a corner. Some quotes were from the course of a real-life day, reminders of moments I remember like they were yesterday:

"Huh. I didn't know you spelled "Cliff Pond" with only one 'f'..."

And some—*"What a time for the dog to learn to talk!"*—with a context I no longer recall, but I laughed at anyway.

All the memories in this! A thirty-year summer camp reunion that I was suddenly in charge of. Where were the details? What was going on that I was cooking for that house party? It wasn't even my house! Or my reunion, for that matter. But, oh my gosh . . . that is the kind of stuff that I love until it hurts and laugh so hard that tears fall. I read all through the journal, and I kept marveling at it. *I remember.* The absurdities of these memories and the magic of them.

As I looked through this miracle of a time capsule, I started to realize what this was. Summer 2012 was my last summer on Cape Cod as a part of Camp Staff. It marked a shift in my life that took me back home to Missouri for the summers. I did have one stray summer working at camp in the years after that, and we still go back for a week here and there for Maggie to go to camp and for me to visit old friends. But this particular summer, this summer of 2012, would certainly have felt more final to me. And I must have wanted to encapsulate its magic. I must have wanted to remember my goodbye. A wistful entry brought me back to a hard-won beginning of wisdom:

> August 6, 2012
>
> Today begins my last week of camp. I am sad, but I am ready for home. I am. I wish I could find some divine reason for why I changed so much over the past five years. Or, more specifically, why my desires for the future changed. I don't know. I don't know that they did. I don't know that they changed as much as they became clear. It became clear to me that I always LOVED going home. Another truth is that I was very depressed after my divorce. VERY. And so my reasoning was a little broken for a long time. Wonderful things came to rescue me, as they sometimes do when everything is falling apart. But it took a long time to put it all back together in a way that made sense to me.

When I finished reading, I took all of these things and packed them back where I found them. In the bag, inside the other bag, and back in the box in the basement. These, the small masterpieces, will stay exactly where I found them. Some things you keep.

You know, when you first go to therapy, you sort of believe everything that comes out of it completely. It's part of why a therapist's code of ethics needs to be so pure. Here, they are entrusted with a person who is wandering around in the emotional dark, and they have to be the hand we hold onto. But as time goes on, I think you start to parse out what truths will stay with you for a time and which you will take with you for the rest of the way. After all, a therapist is only as human as you are . . . and in their defense, the only view they have is the lens through which you see yourself. My therapist from so many years ago once said to me, "I think you try on lives."

Recently, I ran into some old friends while I was running errands, and that put me in mind of my high school years. Another life! Another phase. Another me, as it were. It dawned on me on my way home that possibly I am not a person who "tries on lives." In reality, I am a person with a pretty steady life. One single life with a lot of roots to it. One with many, many pieces that are quite ordinary—and not so very different than twenty other people I could name right off the top of my head.

As I thought back over all these years . . . I traveled through my early life, and then there were the years I worked at a pizza place. The years I put myself through college and my son through his early life by working at Sam's Club on the receiving dock, driving a forklift. The years I began teaching, taking any job that came my way. The Catholic school teacher years. The Cape Cod years. The independent school years. I suppose I could go on. And through all of that, I had her voice in the back of my mind. *I think you try on lives.* Well-intentioned, I think. Surely a correct assessment of some of my choices, yes, but not all of them. Not even most.

To continue to identify myself by this idea that I "try on lives" is to assign myself a careless and cavalier nature, one I do not possess. It suggests a ruthlessness of character that has never been me. Likely, that was not my therapist's intent, though that was how I processed it at the time. That I was cruel. That I was mean to the unsuspecting. It was an assessment that may have fit some things at some times. Possibly. But not so much anymore. And I thought to myself, *Perhaps I don't have to shoulder that load anymore.* Maybe I can forgive myself finally. What I may have been once, I am no longer.

If in one basement box I can find one bag given to me on my birthday by a friend I have had for thirty-seven years, then I am not a woman who tries on lives. If inside that bag is another bag bulging at the seams, containing letters chronicling memories of friends from grade school, high school, and workplaces spanning the past fifteen years . . . then I am not a woman who tries on lives.

If inside that bag there is a book containing priceless memories—even if it's only a slice of them—from people across the country whom I have known and loved, or who have made some deep, unfathomably precious contribution to my life . . . then I am not a woman who tries on lives.

No, I am a woman who tries on LIFE. Between the two is a universe of difference.

22.

the krekel house

If you head west on Highway 70 in Missouri and get off at the Highway K & M exit, take a right onto Highway M, and head down Main Street in O'Fallon, you will eventually roll downhill toward the twin stone churches of Assumption Parish. Passing the Rendezvous Café on your left—which used to be Tom Ginnever's house (locals will recognize the name)—and the old brick McGurk's Public House on your right, you will soon slow down in order to cross over the railroad tracks. There, on your left, you won't be able to miss the Krekel House, which stands sentinel over the town as it has since the late 1800s.

The Krekel House fascinates me. Built around 1867, it refuses to wither. There is a certain proud bearing that resists the ravages of time. No matter how long it stands there, it always looks the same. A little overgrown, but it never sags. Always stands at attention. It's down, but not out. Solitary, but not alone. It needs, but never wants. Somehow it stands there refusing to budge, refusing to bow to the elements.

It captivates me that this house has stood during the Reconstruction era. It has seen Orville and Wilber Wright take flight. It has stood throughout the Roaring Twenties, the invention of the automobile, World Wars I and II. It housed a family during the civil rights movement, Woodstock, the first moon landing, and while the Titanic sank. The abolition of apartheid. The Great Chicago Fire. The invention of the can opener. What this house has seen, the memories it holds . . . I envy it. Not its age—oh no, forty-two is proving to be interesting enough—but its roots. I envy its place in the world. Its place in history.

I have always struggled with a mild sense of displacement in my life. A bit of wanderlust which has given me as many blessings as it's taken. Quite frankly, I've not spent much time aspiring to be the kind of person who lives out her life in one tiny place and never lives beyond it. My mom will tell you that I did aspire to that for a while—and she'd be right—but it was a dream that never quite stuck. I think I coveted that idea in an effort to change my story more than in any sincere effort to live my story.

The house in which I lived longest was my childhood home. When we returned to Missouri, my mom made the decisions which put me solidly in a home—and in a childhood—that I loved.

We lived in Bridgeton, Missouri, on Brookfield Lane. My very best friend, Lynn, lived three doors down. The summers were spent primarily at my house because we had an in-ground pool. The winters were reserved for the sledding-ready hills of her backyard. There was a nearby market that we grew up with and in; a path through the field behind my house was well-worn as our path from home to there. Adults, every one of them, knew our names when we arrived at Klaas Market.

Quite a few members of Lynn's family worked there, so

sometimes we helped them open it in the summer when school was out. Our jobs were small, and likely invented to justify our presence. Counting the copies of the *St. Louis Post-Dispatch*, which is still in circulation, and the issues of the *Globe-Democrat*, which is no longer. I can still remember how hard it was to sacrifice sleeping in on a precious summer morning and how glad I always and ultimately was when we did.

Lynn's mom or sister would always start the coffee for the early-morning customers; Lynn and I would have the giddy and sweet job of pulling the trays of donuts off the pastry truck and counting them to make sure we had the correct amount. Once finished, we each were allowed to choose a single donut, still fresh and warm from the oven. Sitting on the curb of the empty parking lot, we ate our bounty and daydreamed our plans for the rest of the summer that seemed to stretch into forever.

The glow of the sunrise glinting over the acres of fields across the road is a sight that never quite leaves my memory. To this day—nearly every morning—I drink my coffee and wait for the sun. On days when I care to remember it, I can still see us there in that same light. A little sweaty in the early-morning chill. Perpetually a bit sunburned, windblown, mosquito-bit. Miscellaneous scabs and bruises from throwing ourselves at summer: falling off bikes, handsprings and somersaults gone awry. The youngest by far in each of our families, Lynn and I were as beloved as we were irritating and underfoot.

This was our life for all the years of our grade school experience—an unbroken chain of sameness. And then. Lambert Airport wanted to create a buffer zone. Someone somewhere had realized that the planes coming in for landing were, perhaps, a little too close to civilization. So they bought out much of the land surrounding the airfield, and our neighborhood was directly in the path of expansion. We moved. Our house boarded up and scheduled for demolition. And then one day, gone.

I can still remember my mom coming in to my bedroom that day. She had married my stepdad by then, and we moved to the sweetest house in Ferguson, Missouri. She had asked me earlier in the week if I wanted to come with her to see the demolition, and I couldn't fathom that I'd like to see someone take a wrecking ball to my childhood, so I said no. I'm not sure, even now, if I think I should have gone. Maybe it wouldn't haunt me that I never said goodbye in any significant way. To this day, I am heroically awful at goodbyes. Cold, closed, and careless. She brought me back a brick, I do remember that. I kept it on the top shelf of my closet for a long time, though I don't know where it is today.

Lynn and I used to go back sometimes. We'd park on Fee Fee Road and walk past the "Do Not Enter" signs, under the chain barring the entrance. We knew the trees in our respective backyards so intimately and every step of the road from her house to mine. It wasn't hard to pick out where we once were, even though there was only an overgrown field where homes used to be and cracked concrete for a lane. It was a lonely experience that I think we both kind of hated. It was nevertheless a necessary one, and one we doubtless needed to face together. There is an old episode of *The Jeffersons* where Louise goes back to her childhood home before it's going to be knocked down. Just before she leaves, she loosens the glass front doorknob and puts it in her pocket. Sometimes I wish I had a doorknob. I imagine Mom knew that, and that was why she brought me the brick.

I dream about the house from time to time, as Lynn does

about hers. Not always, but sometimes the memories break the surface and return. I wander through it. Sometimes it's spare and dark. Other times, the sunlight still shines through the kitchen window at the exact angle it always did. The phone is still mounted to the cabinet with its mile-long cord. The back door still sounds the same. The same shudder still sticks. I know these things in my mind, though I never touch anything. The walk down the hall feels the same as it always did. No one is there. Nothing is there but me and a vague, sort of disembodied feeling of loss. It's not a sharp, painful feeling—intellectually, I know that my life would have moved on at that juncture anyway since my mom had married right around that time. But something about not having anywhere to come back to had always left a vacancy that I wasn't sure how to fill. And I think Lynn would tell you the same.

You know, people go to therapy, and they are always quick to say, "Oh well, your various problems stem from an unhappy childhood," or what have you. And perhaps that could be true. The adults around us were flawed, to be sure, but they granted to us the best childhood they were able to provide, and one that I remember fondly indeed.

And do I have control issues? Oh, to be sure. But we all do in some capacity. And are they a response to childhood? Indeed. I don't want to belittle all the good work of my therapist all those years ago and the journey we took together. Nor do I want to dismiss all that I have learned about myself through the lens of my choices.

But when I am wandering dream-like through that house and those memories that are long gone, I can't shake a certain feeling that maybe there is another layer unexplored. What if the journey didn't originate from the moments of a childhood that was in some ways troublesome, but instead was born of a childhood that was in so many ways magical, and then gone?

I think the lure of the Krekel House for me was sparked out of the ashes of that. The house stands for a longevity that I don't claim, an endurance that I envy. That there is this house that has such a vast history and has seen generations of a family come and go, live and pass on. That's so inspiring to me. It's hypnotic. Captivating.

The Krekel House has always been in my periphery. I don't think you can live in our town of O'Fallon and not have it be a part of your consciousness in some way. My research, which may not be perfectly correct but is nevertheless dogged, indicates that the original structure was built around the late 1860s. Additions came in the years that followed, and by the 1880s(ish), all parts were enclosed and became what we know today.

Built by Nicholas Krekel, it became the area's first post office in the township of O'Fallon. The railroad depot, O'Fallon Station, is just down the road and still stands today. I can only assume the family lived upstairs, because the main floor housed the railroad agent's office, a general store, and (some reports indicate) even a lending library.

In time, the family expanded. One of Nicholas's daughters married a Westhoff and moved across the way to help him run Westhoff Mercantile, which is the building McGurk's Public House operates out of today. She moved back into the Krekel House later in life, and the house was continuously occupied by the descendants of the Krekel family until the late 1960s.

In the '60s, it changed hands and did a brief stint as an apartment dwelling until it finally became Happy Time Day Care. In 2007, my daughter Maggie attended Happy Time Day

Care, but it eventually closed later that year. With the closing of the day care, the city scooped up the house in an effort to save history, but in 2008, the market crashed. The city of O'Fallon was stuck with it. The Krekel House was closed to the outside world and would remain that way for a decade.

In 2007, many things about my life changed course as well, and many of the doors of me were also closed to the outside world. Oh, I have found many wonders in my life since, ones that I would not give up for the world. I dedicated myself to mothering, daughtering (so to speak), friendship, and creating a home for my kids. Remembering, perhaps, that my mother took the time to do the same for me.

In the intervening years, I created a business called The Winter House which specializes in homemade lotion and has expanded to include all-natural lip balms, insect repellent, homemade soap, and herbal bath salts. It is a labor of love that brings us more friendship and visitors than great business success, but those who imagine that the true definition of wealth is money are the poorer for it.

Since that time, through life and experience, I latched onto the knowledge that I would not be here in this town forever. I chose to do well by my children and make for them the best life possible. But I lost the desire to live life for myself in many ways because the joy I found in living it for others was divine. Standing sentinel and steady for those who needed me.

One night in the late fall of 2016 found Maggie and me at Imo's Pizza on Main Street. Pizza was a must, followed by ice cream. It was a cold day. Rainy. Maybe November, though I can't exactly recall. We were early picking up our pizza, so we commandeered a booth by the door to wait. I had some emails I had to respond to, and I intended to do so. Oddly, my phone—

which was at 37% a minute ago—died. *Poof!* Maggie had forgotten her phone, so in the absence of a screen, we (gasp!) started looking out at the rain and around the restaurant. We moved to another booth to read the information on a historical picture across the room, and from there, I caught sight of the Krekel House on the cover of one of the free circulars that sit on so many of those wire shelves by the doors of businesses around town.

I retrieved it and started reading the article to Maggie. It seemed the house was up for bid. Maggie said, "It could be The Winter House . . . like The *actual* Winter House!" We laughed. Our order was up, and we turned to leave. Maggie ran out to the car through the deluge with half of our order. I tried to put the newspaper back, but something about balancing the pizza, and the soda, and the rain, and the door defeated me, and I ultimately took the paper home, where it mocked us from the kitchen table until I eventually threw it in the recycle bin . . . wait, no . . . in the basket with the bills.

While I didn't imagine life was lucky enough that I would ever own this house, I felt compelled to learn its story. And . . . maybe . . . hope for a miracle. I hope I don't sound melodramatic when I say that I never imagined I would ever stay in the area after Maggie graduates from college, but it had always been a given that I would leave. Until this. This house. The thought of what it could be compelled me. Finally there was something, some purpose of future, that might make me stay.

I was irritated that no one else could see it. How do people drive past it every day, *bump-bump* over the railroad tracks, glance left, and never see that it should hold a family? That, as Maggie said, it should be a place where people gather? Where people take root. A store, or a shop, or a yoga studio below and a home above stairs. The Winter House. If it was mine, I would make it an inn. The Winter House Inn, to be exact. Even with only two rooms, it would never cease to have visitors. The sheer volume of weddings at the—at least—seven churches I can think of off the top of my head would ensure every inn room filled every weekend for every season of the year, save perhaps winter. We have long mourned our imagined non-tourism status here in O'Fallon. But maybe people don't stay in our town because there is nowhere *to stay*. Here is the place. Here. Why can no one see this?

I never bid on the property, though I did start asking questions. I reached out to the people at the city who are, by the way, the most helpful and kind people on the planet. I never denied the fact that I would not be the person qualified to resurrect this house, but that didn't stop me from being willing to . . . oh, I don't know . . . *hope*, I guess. To hope I could be someone who gave my kids those kind of halcyon memories that were given to me. To give my kids the bedrock of the knowledge that this was where they could always find me, instead of coasting on I-don't-knows that I'm tired of.

I hoped these questions could lead me to a miracle, I suppose, or the idea that we would be willing to take on a miracle if it came our way. And in a very real way, though it was in no way that self-sacrificial, I wanted to make enough noise around this house. Enough ripples in the universe that maybe people would wake up. *Pay attention!*

Oh, I wanted this house, to be sure. I wanted the miracle. I wanted what I imagined it could be. I wanted it for my children. For my parents, should one or the other ever need to move in with me in the winter of their own life. I wanted what I loved most—to give people a home when they are far from home.

To host garden parties. Maggie and I dreamed up The Winter House Open House . . . at Christmas. Couldn't you just see the house all decked out in lights? Music spilling out into the street? What a beautiful wondering it was. An open house for those in town. For those I love and for those who have shown me a million kindnesses. To have a family on the lawn again. To have the walls echo with life and adventure and hope and laughter. These things. These things I would have loved.

And writing it now, I know it was huge. It was big and unlikely and foolish and fun. But aren't those things kind of imperative from time to time? My friend, Marcia, always says, "Shoot for the moon. If you do, you'll likely hit the fence post, but if you shoot for the fence post, you'll hit the ground."

But more than any of the other wishes and wonderings came this feeling that finally . . . *finally* . . . after all this time, there was something I wanted for me. Not just for everybody else. Walking through the Krekel House that first day brought back the vestiges of those dream-walks through my childhood home, along with all the other dreams trailing behind me. Something about the house was waiting like I was. Not needing, not desperate. Stoic enough. Solid and peaceful. But waiting. In a way, wanting. All these years, I learned to let go of the desire to want for myself. And suddenly, it returned. I wanted this house. To bring it back to life.

The kids came with me that first day to see the house. It was a strange bit of timing since the three of us are infrequently together. But the kids were so amused by the oddball, ass-backward way I fell into this tour. Not knowing if interest in the house constituted an offer, I told the story one night at dinner, ending with, ". . . long story short, I might have accidentally bought a two-hundred-year-old house."

Delighted, we all showed up on a bright, freezing cold day in December to meet the man from the city charged with leading our tour. Will and I joked that there was a ghost in the house—benevolent, of course—writing his ghost memoirs, "*Someone came to the house today . . .*" This he would write on a freshly turned page of his ghost journal designed just for such a happy occasion.

On the drive there, I told Will that he needed to take pictures while I talked to the agent so I didn't look too interested. Maggie's job was to see if she could tell if it was haunted. A task at which she was ultimately unsuccessful, laughing in the back seat on the way home, "I'm sorry. I couldn't tell if it was haunted . . . I couldn't get my eyeballs to recover from the shocking yellow paint on the walls."

We enjoyed the process so much that I'm afraid I sound as if it was a careless lark. It was not. I would not waste the time of others or the energy and hope of myself or my children in such a reckless and inconsiderate way. It was simply that I expected at any point that the road would end for me, which it eventually did. As I explained it to my friends, "I keep saying no, but the Universe keeps saying maybe. A door opens, and I walk through it, and I will stop when the door remains closed."

I spoke to lawyers. Money managers. City officials. Friends of friends. "I know a guy," became music to my ears. All I wanted was for this to work. A miracle indeed. A friend of mine in real estate helped me decode the proposal paperwork. I have friends who specialize in renovation—particularly historic houses—who walked through the house with me a second time. They looked under the floorboards and found a beam—a 150-year-old tree trunk with the bark still attached that runs the width of the house. The cellar provided no visual evidence of structural damage. They found nooks and crannies, vents where he could show us the old wallpaper that used to line the ceiling. I found out that the house is actually too old for an asbestos problem, and its thirty-five-plus-year stint as a day care rendered the presence of lead paint not a particularly pertinent concern. It was a window into another age, a process that was endlessly fascinating. These, the secrets of a house simply waiting.

"Oh, it's a job, for sure," my friend Jason admitted as we stood outside at the curb. He is a contractor who specializes in historic houses.

"You need new plumbing. New electric. But anybody going in knows that." Drywall. Insulation. Wiring. All this needs to be new.

"Still," he said. "It's a good house. A solid house." A solid house for any house, I am to understand, let alone one that is 150 years old.

While I would adore the story if it ended with me being able to fulfill a lifelong dream of rehabbing an old house, we all know that sometimes dreams are only that. The reality of my life does not include the financial wherewithal to get into this house. While I could surely maintain it if it was livable, the road to the process is paved with currency I do not possess. But I tried, and I learned a lot, and I love that.

And the thing is? It's okay. Whatever dream I knit around this house wasn't going to return to me what was lost. I think that's a fallacy we live out, that we can ever put it all back together. That with enough control, or opportunity, or money, or distance, or security, we'll be able to recover our losses— whatever they may be or ever were. And I was sad when the obvious futility of this hope was revealed to me. Sure, I was.

But it was a sadness of my own making. And—like so many things in life—we contribute to our own misery by perceiving our losses through the lens of the best of what they could have been instead of the truth of what they very realistically would have been. As for me? I shall return to my world as I have made it, making the best home I can for these two miracles I have already asked for and have been granted.

Besides. I'll let you in on a secret: These spring rains that just pummeled us here in central Missouri, and made the creek rise and rush through the woods in my backyard, reminded me in a New York minute what happiness there is to be found in a newly built house. The rain lashing at my windowpane does not keep me awake at night wondering where the wet-vac is, praying that—come morning—I won't be airing out the basement rug. Blessings arrive in life in so many different ways. Some reveal themselves quite clearly, and still others wait for the perfect rainy-day circumstance to shine.

{Author's Note: Three months after the original publication of this blog post, the Krekel House was sold. It was renovated and refurbished lovingly, returned to its original glory. It is currently a bridal shop. To honor its place in history and its service to our town, the shop was christened, "Cleo Bridal at The Krekel House."}

23.

the winter house

It's so funny to me the things you remember about yourself and the things you leave behind for others to keep. Maggie came up to me the other day, as I stood at the stove making gravy, and said, "I hope you know that cornstarch is poisonous."

I said, "No it isn't! What are you talking about?"

She laughed and said, "Don't you remember? That one time I used cornstarch to make my lip gloss a matte finish? I came down to show you, and I was all impressed with myself. You listened and then said, with a totally straight face, 'You know cornstarch is poisonous, don't you?'"

Needless to say, I had completely forgotten that. It's nice to have someone remind you of laughs gone by. And tonight? The same thing happened. But kind of different.

I was on the phone with my mom in Florida. She was sewing a baby quilt, and I was making lotion. Each of us had the other on speaker. We talked about the holiday parties she attended, her new friends, old friends. Family. Life. Community. The stuff of mother-daughter conversations.

She said, "Are you making lotion right now?"

I said, "Yep. Twenty-four jars tonight."

She said, "That is amazing! And to think it all started with that medical bill."

I paused in my whipping. "That's *right* . . . I had totally forgotten that!"

A few years ago, Maggie got her arm caught on a handrail partition at the airport in Providence, Rhode Island. She managed to get her arm unstuck, but when she went to step toward me, she fainted. Something about white blood cells rushing to the location of her now fractured wrist. She quickly came to, but the ambulance was called. Randomly passing out in the airport is, apparently, frowned upon by the airlines, and one is not allowed to immediately get on an airplane after that. Airlines want a wee bit of assurance that this passenger isn't medically compromised. So, as it happened, our luggage was dragged out of the belly of the plane. We were rushed out of the airport, she on a gurney, and tore through the streets of Providence on our way to the emergency room. All was well. We took a later flight out that evening after assuring she was safe to fly.

Months went by. School started. The bill came in. Even splitting it with her dad as was our parenting agreement—it was too much.

I was recalled to the present when Mom said, "I was telling this man at the holiday party about your lotions. I said to him, 'She had to pay this medical bill, but she didn't have the money. She called me and said to me, 'Mom—'"

"*I need to find a way to turn one dollar into two . . .*" I suddenly remembered. "I totally forgot that I said that to you!"

One day, right around the time that the medical bill came in, the head of the independent school where I worked came into my classroom. I happened to be putting on hand lotion at the time, and she needed some. I passed her the jar of lotion that I had for my family. Just an old mixture. This and that. It was cheaper than premade lotion and had the added benefit of being made with more natural ingredients. She loved it! And as the days went on, she would pop in and grab the lotion whenever she needed some.

One day in November, she said, "How much would you charge me for that?"

I said, "I don't know. Five dollars, I guess? I could just tell you how to make it."

She said, "I don't want you to tell me how to make it. I want you to make it for me, slap a label on it, and I want to give it to people as gifts. I think people would buy this."

I went home that weekend. No label. No idea what to call this lotion. But I loved the idea that it came out of our house, and I wanted to honor that. We had always rented a summer cottage on Cape Cod in the summer, thus we had long dubbed our house in Missouri "The Little Winter House."

That weekend, as the kids and I sat eating lunch at our kitchen table, I asked Will, "Do you think I should call this lotion company 'The Little Winter House'?"

He thought. "No," he said. "Just 'The Winter House.'" He happened to be taking a marketing class in college at the time. "People like three words in a name, not four."

". . . and I said to the man," Mom continued her story on the phone, "'so she knew she made this lotion and a couple of people had liked it. So she thought maybe a couple more people would like it . . . and she turned it into a company! And my granddaughter makes lip balms and sells them under her own little company as well. They don't make a whole lot of money, but my daughter always says they consistently turn one dollar into two, and that's all she ever asked for.'"

Truth be told, I'm not really telling this story for me. It is my favorite story to tell for everyone else. I tell it for Maggie. I tell it for Will. So they can see that even the falls and breaks can lead to greater things. Things they never even considered. So they can see that even one word or two at a lunch table or one conversation in the middle of a random day can make all the difference in the world if you are paying attention.

Success in life is variable. One person's definition may not be another's. But your success, whatever it may be . . . it comes in pieces. Gather them. Listen. Pay attention. The picture is there, you just have to put the pieces together.

24.

auld lang syne

Writers are taught (and rightfully so) that the first paragraph of any document needs to be an attention grabber. Grab the reader's attention . . . grab it! If you don't have it in the first paragraph—maybe even the first line—then you don't have it at all. But I don't have any handy stylistic paragraph that starts with a bang. Or a question. Or a fancy quote to hook you. I have only this: It starts with an old friend on my doorstep at Christmastime.

Diane and I used to work together at a school in Florissant. It is one of the few schools in North County which is still open to this day and still bears its original name. She had worked at the school for quite a while, her own children having been brought up in it. I swung into employment there around 2008 on the tail end of a period of my life which—in hindsight—was my downfall and my salvation all at once.

It was a crazy place. A madhouse. Thirty-three-plus kids in a classroom with one teacher. A principal who, while not without her goodness, was a bit of a kook herself and quite a sycophant to the parents, which never bodes well for the staff. She was a yeller. A blamer. And she would do both to you and in front of parents. She didn't do it to me, but I think that was because she felt sorry for me. The downfall, as you recall. I never had enough to wear, nor enough to eat. She gave me a lot of socks. She frequently found coats. And extra food.

Looking back, obviously she bought them for me, but at the time, I was convinced it was God simply looking out for me. And perhaps He was. The thing that has been the hardest for me to learn in life is that people aren't just one thing. Wrong *once* doesn't mean wrong *always*. A protagonist in your story can be an antagonist in the life story of someone else. We're all just connected like that.

Diane came over one night last week to pick up her Winter House order. Years have gone by since I've seen her. People have come and gone in my life. Her kids have moved up and out. I've had two different jobs, and two different houses. But the sound of the doorbell energized me, and when I swung the door open, there she stood. The same. Oh, so every bit exactly the same, and I was thrown back in time to that madhouse place and the hundreds of foxhole memories we shared.

As Diane and I sat at my table on a freezing cold night in December drinking tea, we remembered all the craziness. All the dysfunction. The music teacher playing the saxophone in the hallway. Cool . . . but why? The admin from New Zealand who would dress the kids down like nobody's business. The time the principal tried—at an assembly, no less, with parents present—to put a moratorium on the kids saying "boujee" because she didn't know what it meant. All the times we laughed until we cried, and sometimes just plain cried, in the break room.

"Remember that gigantic corkboard that only ever had that one tiny comic strip on it? The one with the—"

"The Parent-Teacher Conferences!" we both screamed at the same time.

It was a picture of two parents on one side of a desk. The teacher, on the other side of the desk, is saying, "*Yes. I know your son is a genius. And clever too for hiding it so well.*" It was the only thing that ever made its appearance on the acre of cork surrounding it, which was somehow a metaphor for our lives there, though I don't know what the metaphor was.

We remembered Betty, whom I ran into in the Target parking lot last year at Christmas. Betty is now retired and still bears a striking resemblance to Betty White in all the ways that matter: she has a wicked sense of humor, and she has white hair. Plus, you know . . . *her name.* Beyond that, she was so kind. She worked so hard. She believed in kids when there was nothing left to believe in.

Betty once had a student named Jonathan who took to dropping the f-bomb in third grade. His parents, when confronted with the problem, told the principal that he "must have learned it from his teacher" because they do not talk like that in their house. The principal believed them and confronted Betty.

Betty.

Betty, who wouldn't have said "Boo!" to a ghost. She related the whole story to us that day at lunch—and there was nothing for it . . . we laughed and laughed and laughed. What else were we going to do? It positively defied understanding. It was outlandish. Preposterous. I couldn't wrap my head around it. Betty was horrified and near tears, so we all tried to bolster her spirits and the conversation moved on.

I told of a recent development in my own life. A story about a guy they all knew of—a frequent and unfortunate character in my life—who wasn't very nice to me. He seemed to only be interested when I was walking away, a pattern that I was somehow helpless to put an end to. I said that he had texted me the night before, out of the blue. They asked how I handled it, and I responded:

"Well, I just said to him: *'What do you want now, motherfucker?'*" Then I looked around the table. "You know . . . like Betty would say."

And, I mean . . . it brought the house down.

That's not actually what I said to the guy. Not ever anything I *would* say, but it made Betty laugh so hard that it was well worth spitting those words out the mouth I kiss my mother with. And it gave birth to Betty's and my favorite inside joke—that I would randomly string together the foulest, most offensive collection of curse words I could think of . . . the nastier the better . . . and every time, I'd preface it by saying, "Like Betty would say . . ."

People will tell you that you need to fight everything. You need to go toe to toe on every slight, every wrong, every injustice. You don't. Well . . . you do and you don't. It's a balancing act. You need to not be apathetic, for sure—if I've learned anything over the years, it is that apathy to injustice is just as unattractive as outright meanness. But you can't fight everything. And in this school—we couldn't fight the administration. The controlling principal. The apathetic priest.

All we could do was laugh to dispel the misery and make community of each other.

In the movie *The American President*, one of the characters says to another, "You fight the fights that need fighting!" But there are enough people, and enough fights, that you don't need to fight every one of them. And in this school, the fight was not with the administration. The fight that needed fighting was for the kids.

For Betty, it was a boy, so angry by eight years of age. What would the world do with him if she didn't teach peacefulness?

For me, it was Faith, who lost her mother at birth and was being raised by her grandmother. A woman who came in at least once a week saying, "Oh, I need your help with this girl, Ms. Mudd. I need your help and the Lord's help . . . in that order." Faith, who had the sweetest laugh . . . so sweet that I loved to make up outlandish stories about how I went to a carnival in the school's basement while she was out at recess and now my belly hurt from all that cotton candy. She would roll out that bubbly giggle and say, "Ms. Mudd . . . you telling stories again!"

Faith, whom I kept snacks in my drawer for and Ziploc bags in my desk for the times she'd come up to my desk flummoxed and holding her hair.

"Ms. Mudd! My weave just fell out!" and we'd place it in a Ziploc and send it home to Titi. Faith, who called my hair "magic hair" because it moved. What is the world going to do to a little girl who looks in the mirror and doesn't see her own beauty?

My fight was for Isaac, who we joked that—even in first grade—he tried to hit on all the teachers. He'd give a smooth, little chin pump to you as he walked in the classroom in the morning and say,

"How you doing today, Ms. Mudd?"

"I'm fine, Isaac, how are you?"

"I'm good, Ms. Mudd. I'm real good today."

I always said that Isaac was going to be the Smooth Hits Late Night DJ . . . he reminded me so much of that old SNL

Ladies' Man skit with Tim Meadows. What a doll. And my fight was for him . . . that the world would turn out to be every bit as awesome and hopeful as he thought it was. Every day a new fresh start.

Soon, Diane had to go home, and I had to start getting ready for bed. Five A.M. comes early. She grabbed her lotion order and headed out. I made sure she knew the way out. Made sure I told her to have a Merry Christmas.

There are some times in life that I call "litmus experiences." That is to say, they set up the comparison for all the encounters you have after it. And, though they may be difficult, they serve a purpose. Ever after, you are able to look at your present circumstances and say, "This is difficult, yes, but it isn't as difficult as *that* was." So you find you are a better person for having endured it. Or them. The litmus experiences of your life.

And the true beauty of them . . . once you are far enough away from them . . . is that, in retrospect, they reveal an even greater life truth. I often tell my kids that the devil is so loud in this world because he knows he's losing. And meanness, crassness, unkindness, exclusion . . . these things are loud. Clanging. Self-congratulating. And in their arrogance, they reveal the fundamental truth of their fear. Because in the end, these things secretly know what we know out loud: That love wins.

Fear? Anger? Pride? These things are poison from the start. They are their own downfall, and we need not concern ourselves with them. They don't matter. They don't last.

This fall, I was staying with friends in Dallas during the weekend of the OU/TX game. I woke up that Sunday morning to a Facebook message that came to me from out of the past.

"*Dear Ms. Mudd*," it read. "*It's Rita Jones, mother of one of your first-grade students in 2008. I reached out because Halla has not ever stopped thinking about you or talking about you . . . thanks for giving her a wonderful experience in first grade. She said you were her favorite teacher. Your students are blessed to have you.*"

And I guess that was the starting point of me really looking back at the years I worked at that school, a retrospective which culminated with my old friend at my door. Drinking tea at my kitchen table.

So many memories. So many faces. So many sweet peas. So much love in each classroom—even as dysfunction swirled around us. Looking back on the sort of oddball nightmarish quality of that experience, Diane and I could only remember the foibles of it intellectually. Not the feeling of it. Nor the despair. In the end, the only thing we took with us was the good. In the end, you are only cloaked in the good you've done. See it in yourself as others see it on you.

25.

in your time

What a blessing of a day today is already. We have an "Ice Day," so we're all settled at home. So thrilling. The world waits. Well—not the *world*. That's a little grandiose. Perhaps only the city waits. The region. Still, it's so silent, isn't it? Like we are cocooned. I'm watching squirrels in the backyard. They are so busy where I am not. They gather food, and I gather thoughts. Silence pushes to the forefront the important things.

I often think of the swirling bounty of the universe around me. It's important to me to be grateful and never to get caught up in the habit of *more*. But it's a struggle for me as it is for everybody. The desire for more is such a very human weakness. Still, the way the universe ebbs and flows and has delivered so much bounty to me convinces me, more than ever, that the universe—or God, whichever distinction makes you feel the sense of your blessings— does not heed your words, or your prayers, or even your actions, but only the small secret language of your motivation.

I'm convinced that the universe listens to your spirit, not the trappings of your humanity. It is only the powerful combination of true belief, pure motivation, and authentic desire that propels the universe into action. And, in no small part, a kind of acceptance of whatever becomes of those things about you which are true. Not control. No, never that. You don't control God or the Universe through these characteristics, and you cannot fabricate them.

Think about it. We, as humans, feel falseness. A lie you feel in your solar plexus region. Unkindness we feel in our stomachs. We know the truth of people whether or not they are even aware of it themselves. Why would the universe be less powerful than us? If our own bodies can sense a disingenuous intent, then why wouldn't the universe be able to?

We like to say things happen "in God's time," and that's always been such a weird turn of phrase to me. What a thankless task to be assigned the timeline, like the poor soul at work who's in charge of the schedule.

That, and I'm always horrified by the whole "God's will" concept during times of tragedy. I think it's well-intentioned, but it just never hit its mark with me. I think to myself, *Really? This is God's will? Because if it is, then you must think that guy is a real bastard.* I mean, if these things comfort you and bring you genuine peace, then by all means, feel free to keep them around. I am not disparaging them as a concept—they just never landed on me right in any of my hours of need.

For me, the truth of the matter is this: It *is* God's time. But not because He's controlling it. It's God's time only in the sense that He's the only one who knew the hour of my arrival. God isn't slow to react, but I am slow in getting to the moment when the action is taking place. My path is littered with my own flaws and distractions and fears, so it takes a while to get there.

I just can't imagine that God took time away from whatever He does all day long to place a giant Divine thumbtack on any of our timelines and hold happiness away from us until then.

No, of course not. The moment of any particular life bounty and its distance from me is determined not by the Universe, not by God, but by the pace of *my own* progress. God's not been moving the finish line, He's been waiting for me there. And the moment I arrive—stressed out and late, willing to listen and finally cracked open enough to be filled—is the time the universe will pour out its blessings.

This is the time, and not a single moment sooner, because that's how long it took me to get to this place where I pulled together the various strings of my life's passions and formed them into one message.

This is the time when, through all my foibles and fumbles, I managed to stumble into the discovery of what I really wanted my life to look like. This is the time when life made clear to me my path.

This is the time when I accepted that there are decisions I don't feel like making and processes I don't feel like doing, but the fear of doing them became less than the fear of what would become of me if I didn't do them.

This is the time when my prayers for clarity stopped being thrown out into the universe, or up to the Divine, and when I realized that they need to take root within.

This is the time when I realized that God was the hand I held and the universe was the anchor I counted on, but I finally accepted that the work was my own. And until the authenticity and the openness of that was born in me, until the clarity of that propelled me fearlessly forward, until I realized that the various and assembled ropes and chains and pieces of my life were not a broken collection, but rather the supplies to make a bridge to a me that was better—then God's time *couldn't* come to pass. Because it never was God's time at all. It was always mine.

26.

fine, indeed

My grandpa was an artist, a ceramics maker, a "damn liar" if my grandmother was to be believed, and quite an avid fisherman. An irresistibly charming man was Harry Belgeri, and one who inspired a trail of love everywhere he went.

As the story goes, he met my grandma when she was seventeen. He was from an Italian family who ran a tavern on the Italian side of town, and he was expected to marry a "nice Italian girl." I'm not sure how he met my grandma, but after he did, he told his family that he couldn't fulfill their plans. Telling them simply, "I'm sorry. I just can't get my mind off a little Irish girl."

When he was around forty years old, Grandpa was diagnosed with cancer of the larynx. Soon after the diagnosis, he had his larynx removed, as it was determined that was the only course of action to stop the spread of the cancer. It has always amazed me that it actually worked. In 1965, when what they knew about cancer could probably fit into a thimble compared with today's dearth of information, but it worked. Grandpa went on to live for thirty-eight more years, meeting all eight of his grandchildren and Will, his first great-grandchild.

In light of this new reality, Grandma and Grandpa had to reverse the cultural roles of the '60s. Grandma went back to school, became a registered nurse and the primary breadwinner in their home. Grandpa became the homemaker. By the time my mom and I moved in with them in 1979, he was well-entrenched in his role. He cooked dinner and did the laundry and ironing. He kept up the house and maintained the swimming pool in our backyard. He ran the carpool and always made sure my school uniform was clean and ready. He did the grocery shopping and was a beloved character at our local market with all the deli ladies who loved nothing more than to take care of him.

After the laryngectomy, Grandpa taught himself to talk again without the use of any type of device, though it took him some time. He was able to make himself understood best to his family, but was generally successful in other places over the course of time. To understand him required a discriminating ear we never realized we had until we were surprised into the position of translating to strangers. Like a person with a stammer, he would become harder to understand if he was upset or frustrated. As a result, he was a calm man, but I can remember a time or two when it became necessary to rest a settling hand on his arm and speak for him. His was a language we knew by heart, a most beloved crushed-gravel voice and the *tck-tck* clicking sound of his laughter.

My mom once met a man at a party who had a laryngectomy. The woman who hosted the party thanked her afterwards for talking to the man all night long, saying, "I feel bad when he isn't involved in conversations, but it is so hard to understand him."

Mom said, "Not for me. For me it was a chance to talk to my dad again."

Grandpa's hobby was to mix, cast, paint, and fire ceramics. We had a kiln in our garage, which made it one of the warmest places in our house in the dead of winter. Many days he could be found in his garage workshop casting molds or at the kitchen table painting tiny details on Christmas village houses. These were a popular holiday gift from him to those he loved, and I have many a memory of searching the gritty shelves of the ceramics store for a new addition to the village set: a shoe cobbler's house, a bakery, a Victorian couple skating. A boy selling papers. A one-room schoolhouse. Worlds of wonder were contained along those concrete aisles.

One year, he made ceramic swans as gifts. Delicate, feminine. Fluid columns of unrelieved alabaster white. Another year, he made wreaths to adorn the mantels and decorative shelves of all his loved ones. Painted a glossy evergreen, these wreaths have holes dotted along the surface in which you can nestle plastic colorful pegs to simulate Christmas lights.

Bloop. Bloop. Bloop. Like bubbles breaking on the surface of water, he poked holes in the wet ceramic cast with the point of a toothpick. I stood on my dusty stool and watched him, and he would look down at me and smile.

I can still hear him now. "How does it look, babe?" he would ask. And I would tell him it looked fine indeed.

But five/six/seven-year-old me had no sense of the challenge this created for thirty- and forty-year-old me. Thoughtful though it may have been, the particular genius of Harry Belgeri did not *quite* extend to completing this project in a way that made it functional. This wreath. You remember, the nestling holes for the peg lights are the diameter of a *toothpick*. And a toothpick . . . well, it doesn't create a hole wide enough to fit the base of the pegs. So. Every year it came out. Every year it graced the house. And every year it shined in my memory, but not in reality.

Finally, years upon years later, I found another man to complete what was started a lifetime ago. One winter night, he sat. Dremel in hand, Dan calmly, painstakingly drilled out each of those wreath holes. Delicate ceramic, a piece at least thirty-five years old. Carefully, his artistic eye never wavered, his work-calloused hands precise and steady.

Once, I asked my grandpa how he knew the cancer wouldn't come back, a question which strikes my adult ears as insensitive and careless, but I was young. Probably eight or so. He thought for a second and then said, "Well, babe. I guess I'll know the cancer didn't come back when I die of a heart attack . . . and probably not a moment sooner than that." What a free fall into the arms of life that was! To ride on the wings of pure faith, it's a statement as mind-blowing to me now as it was the day I heard it.

In the final years of his life, he had a series of strokes which left him silent again. The muscles he needed to speak were weakened, his words were barely a breath and then not even that. And I don't know why I failed him the way that I did. It was so hard for me to see him like that, and I didn't visit him in his waning years as often as I should have. Foolish of me to waste such precious time. There are some decisions in life you just take with you, and these are the heaviest of mine.

I'm not even sure I cried at his funeral. It was such a profound loss to me, unreachable by tears. In so many ways, he was the only heart I really knew. To make up for failing him at the end of his life, I can only clearly remember wanting to sing him home.

When I walked out of the church, Lynn was waiting at the bottom of the steps for me. Upon seeing her there, alone, one hand on her rounded eight-month belly, a sound escaped. A deep welling of a sound that proved to be the cork that held back everything else. Some angel of grace carried me down the steps safely to her, and I remember her stepping a foot backward to contain the momentum of my arrival. I'm not sure how long we stood like that—me crying on her shoulder and she holding on tight.

Into the moments that followed, one small voice entered.

"*Damn it.*"

I laughed a little, though who could say how I had it in me. A sniff, wipe your tears, watery kind of laugh, and I looked up at my grandma who had materialized at Lynn's shoulder.

"*Mrs. Belgeri . . .*" Lynn reached out a hand and started to express her condolences, a moment arrested by—

"Look at this!" Grandma gestured disgustedly skyward, an impatient flap of her hand.

"That *jackass,*" she tried to say with passion, but her voice contained a sharp wobble of a different emotion. We three looked up where the flakes were starting to drift down.

"He did this on purpose," she told us. "He always knew I hated the snow . . ."

Somehow just the thought of him right then—being purposefully in the moment with us, right on the other side of the veil—arrowed straight to my heart. The thought of his grin, that sly, teasing look in his eye—*tck-tck*, he would laugh. Or maybe now in heaven he was finally free to laugh out loud again. A great, hearty sound I had never heard.

"*I'm sorry, babe,*" he would tease my grandma as he had a thousand times, "*but you're so beautiful when you're mad.*"

And, oh how the three of us stood on those stone steps and *laughed*. Laughed to make sense of the grief, I suppose. My grandma, she always knew. She always knew what a moment needed. I don't know that she cried at the funeral either—she and I, we were sisters in strength.

In the years following Grandpa's death, we found a letter among his things. A typed submission to *Reader's Digest* entitled "My Year of Silence," recalling his journey to make the decisions that would change his life, but also keep his life. It was an insight to him I had never considered, to see the struggle of a scared father of six children taking on the prospect of a terrifying surgical procedure. I don't know if it was ever published. It would be just like him—to publish something and never tell a soul.

Six months after Grandpa's funeral, I turned thirty years old. On the day of my thirtieth birthday party, my grandma arrived with my aunt Katie. I was four months pregnant with Maggie at the time. We hugged, said our hellos, and Katie headed off to greet other family members in the backyard. I was surprised to feel Grandma put something cold in the palm of my hand. Then she folded my fingers over it and patted my fist, as was her way. I opened my hand to reveal a ring. One he had given her on their thirtieth wedding anniversary. Silver, maybe white gold. Small stones, probably not worth that much on the open market, but priceless to me.

"He always loved you the most," she said.

It makes me smile, now, to remember a night not long ago when we were at Dan's brother's house for his nephew's birthday party. I was in the kitchen with Dan's sister-in-law, Meghan, and another woman whom I had deduced was their neighbor—but who was also either Meghan's cousin or her best friend. Possibly both.

Meghan and I were talking, and the other woman stood at the counter, listening. When I finished telling a funny story about Dan, the woman blurted, "Okay-I-have-to-know," strung together as one rapid-fire word. "So you and Dan *are* dating? *Have been* dating . . . ?"

"*Ohmygosh!* I'm sorry!" Meghan told her neighbor/friend/cousin. "I assumed you had been introduced."

"*Yes*," Meghan confirmed for her. "This is Mona. She and Dan have been dating for a while."

She smiled at me. "It seemed like it, but I didn't want to ask. Dan seems like he un-dates people kind of . . . fast."

"Ohmygosh, no," said Meghan, her glass of wine lending her words either more truth or more nonsense. Nevertheless, her next sentence warmed my heart.

"Dan loves Mona . . . like . . . more than he's ever loved anyone in his entire life."

Dan glances up at me only briefly before returning to work on the wreath, and I smile, my memories in so many places at once. I consider myself blessed, indeed, to be loved so well by two such men.

In the whir of the hand tool, I can see the work of tiny drill bits expanding the holes slowly, patiently, and precisely. Dan is also a caretaker. He owns his own windshield business, but his heart beats with a different kind of soul. He is a cook, he's an artist. The table he works at is one he built for me. Many nights I come home from an exhausting workday to the scent of dinner on the stove. He waits with a comfort he reserves just for me. The lyrics of a song by the Dixie Chicks find me in that moment:

I've come to find refuge in the easy silence that you make for me;
It's okay when there's nothing more to say to me.
In the peaceful quiet you create for me;
And the way you keep the world at bay for me.

I adore the sight of him. His wide shoulders hunkered over one of my most precious gifts, an object containing a treasure of memories.

"How does it look, babe?" he asks without stopping his work.

And I tell him it looks fine indeed.

27.

mine all mine

One long-ago summer, though I can no longer remember which one, I was sitting on a counter-stool in a friend's kitchen, lingering over coffee and picking at a donut from The Hole in One in Orleans, Massachusetts. We were talking about people. Personalities. She spoke of this theory centering around the concept of Enlightenment. She had read a book or had taken a class. I can't remember anymore how it was she came by this information. The theory was that there is a spectrum of enlightenment. The spectrum, which transcends socioeconomic standing, race, culture, religion, and any other categorizing factors, spans from zero to seven. Zero being a newborn baby. Seven being Jesus, Muhammad, Gandhi, Mother Teresa . . . people like these.

She said that most people are propelled higher up the scale through tragedy, but some people can move up through choice. The more difficult of the movement styles is choice, not because tragedy is easy, but because tragedy changes you without your permission. You have been irrevocably altered. Period. But to move up the . . . "ladder" by choice? Ah, well. That involves the strength of your will, which is only as powerful a tool as you require it to be.

To understand this philosophy, you have to realign some of your basic understandings of order and progression. Even my allusion to a "ladder" is sort of a baseline cultural one and doesn't do justice to the purity of the concept. It implies that you are going up—which assumes that there also would be a way down, which is incorrect because you don't go "down" at all. You start, and then you either progress or you don't. You move forward, or you remain still. The ladder visual also puts us in the mind frame of there being souls who are above and "better" than you, or below and "worse" than you. That's not right. In fact, the concept of comparison, on any level, is not the correct headspace of this idea. This is an individual endeavor and not dependent upon the progress of others.

As we acquaint ourselves with this space, we find Stage Zero to be the beginning of life, not a lack of goodness or purity, it's just simply the beginning. Stage One would be comprised of mainly young children. Again, not that they lack *goodness*, but that they lack *enlightenment*. Remember that the spectrum isn't quantifying goodness or innocence, but enlightenment and your progression along a spiritual journey. Young children are in the primary stages of cognitive development. Emotionally and socially, their perception of life is very egocentric. They ascribe to philosophies like: *If I have to do it, you have to do it*. Say things like, "That's not fair." Anything that you would normally hear out of the mouths of grade-schoolers or middle schoolers.

These are the children, and in some cases adults, who say staggeringly hurtful things, often unaware of their effect on others. If, by some bit of grace, they are made aware of their effect, they will likely exempt themselves from the responsibility of their words or actions by blaming you or your behavior. *I wouldn't have done it if you wouldn't have made me mad.*

These people are concerned a lot with fairness as it pertains to them, but lack the accompanying concept of how it may pertain to others. Cognitively, this stage has the potential to wear off in grade school, as people move out of egocentricity into an awareness of the outside world looking in. But, in truth, the theory suggests that many adults have never progressed beyond this group. Their desires or narratives have become more sophisticated as they've aged, but their true belief system remains rooted in Stage One.

As we progress through and out of school age, and out of Stage One into Stage Two, we move into an awareness of the world beyond the end of our noses. So enters the concept of comparison. It's a one-two punch that awareness of the outside world looking in coincides with adolescence . . . what a sucker punch, right? On the heels of this enters the realization that people are different. We begin to group the differences with headings: popular people, rich people, poor people, mean girls, jocks, geeks, etc.

In and of itself, this is not a bad thing. This is actually a pretty brain-based exercise. Our brains like to chunk in order to process information faster. Remember that the brain is an incredibly complex machine with one very simple task: survival. As such, it likes to scan, it likes to chunk, it likes to put things in order.

Your brain only has seven pieces of working memory at a time. Think of seven Post-it notes. If there is anything you can chunk onto one note, then that leaves your brain open to process more. It's the reason that teachers want their students to memorize their multiplication facts. If you don't know that six times seven equals forty-two, then the reach for that information is occupying five of those precious seven Post-its, so you've only got two spaces left to learn anything new.

On the other hand, if you know the answer and can put forty-two on one Post-it, then you've got a lot more working memory to use to learn a new concept. So chunking, itself, is a brain operation, and there's not a whole lot you can do about that even if you wanted to.

Putting things in order is also very brain-based. The only danger of chunking and ordering is when you take a very primitive operation and use it as permission to assign value to either yourself or others. Or when you start moving them around to position yourself better.

Stage Two finds folks a little more advanced, but still predominantly concerned with where they are on the ladder of ordering things. They are still concerned with fairness, from a standpoint of flat-rate equality, but some even extend into the higher-functioning concept of equity. But still, it is where a "Keeping up with the Joneses" lifestyle exists. This is where a culture of blame exists. Where competitive thinking exists. Stage Two people aren't completely egocentric, but there is still a marked preoccupation with the self. People who define themselves by their looks and possessions.

Notice that I said "defined by." *Enjoying* something is not the same as being defined by it. Enjoying your looks and sprucing them up for your own enjoyment is a wonderful thing. That can boost your confidence in a really, really healthy way. Additionally, wanting to love your home, and feathering your nest with pretty things, or enjoying a drive in a luxurious car . . . these are not drawbacks. I couldn't say where anyone else is on the Enjoyment/Defined By continuum, and it's not for me to do so. You know in your heart where you are, and you're the only one who needs to know. But still, the hallmark of this stage is a self-narrative that needs a comparison to be completed. And what does this sound like to you? Sounds like high school to me.

Now, don't get me wrong, an adolescent can be well beyond Stage Two. Absolutely. Especially given any lessons they have had to learn in their life so far. This spectrum is not bound by age. But when we collectively think of a preoccupation with self, looks, social standing . . . we think *high school*.

As we moved along in our conversation, my friend eventually said—and this *blew my mind*—that most people live their entire lives and never progress farther than Stage Two. Can you imagine?! *Two!* Out of *seven*!! Personally, I think what makes Stage Two so hard to move beyond is that it's really hard to get past all the forms of comparison. And what is the basis of all forms of comparison? The Big Seven. This is where Greed lives. Envy. Wrath. The Seven Deadly Sins, right? Sloth. Lust—though I'm convinced that if this one's wrong, I don't really want to be right. Gluttony. Pride. These are beasts. These are hard to resist. Greater souls than I have struggled with the chains of these Seven.

"Can you be a Three with some people and not everyone?" I asked, because let's be honest, I'm a little more selfless on behalf of my kids than I am on behalf of, say, the postman.

She said, "No." Just *No*.

Honestly, I guess you do have the ability to be better with some people than others, but within the frame of this thought process, that doesn't make you enlightened. After all, what does the Bible say? Something about even sinners being kind to those who are kind to them. I didn't love that theory, in general, and I really was not impressed with myself through this lens.

But, for better or worse, it lit a fire in me—this idea. A fire to be something better. And, failing that, a fire to at least *try to be* something better. I remember thinking, as clear as a bell,

Well, I will be damned if I leave this earth without being at least a Three, and so a journey began: a journey to Three.

What became clear to me very early on was that this had to be real work. This was not the-front-pew-on-Sunday and judgmental and superior the other six days of the week. It had to be pure. It had to be honest. And the hardest person to be honest with is, of course, yourself.

I started to realize that the likely reason this type of change grows more abundantly out of the hearts and ashes of tragedy is because there is no ego associated with tragedy. It's part of why it is so painful. Just because I chose this journey, rather than tragedy plunging me into it, didn't negate the fact that its growth within me was still going to come from a place of pain. I simply couldn't grow through this process and hold onto my ego at the same time.

The thing that comes first, that *has to come first*, is the death of the ego. Death of the false parts—and you have to be willing to admit what those false parts are. It's a slow, tragic demise of the narrative you use to cloud your real story. Death to the part that scans for where blame can be placed outside of you. Death to the part that searches for the way you can be superior in thought or action.

The thing is, I so desperately wanted this journey to be about the moment where I meet others, but it's not. It's about the place where I meet myself. The bare me. The only real me. The shards and the broken pieces, the raw edges, and even the tattered leftovers that had somehow remained intact. I wanted to find a way to take that stuff and leave the rest. But it required an honesty that was . . . *honestly?* . . . painful.

At first, I thought this would be accomplished by taking up more space. Making myself bigger. I took on more things.

Fighting the fight. Arguing point, for point, for point. Marking my territory and making sure everybody knew where I thought they stood on theirs. I tried to be everything to everybody. I made a lot of noise. Telling my story from the rooftops and giving away the pieces of me and all of my moments to make other people happy. Bleeding on the page. Giving, giving, giving my heart. Even to people who, frankly, didn't want it. I gave until there was no more to give, and if I had nothing left, I convinced myself it was because I deserved it. And at the time, I had a lot of people around me who were willing to echo that. But then I realized: *Wait. That's not right.* And also around that time, a good friend said to me, "I don't think love means being emotionally terrified all the time." And she was right, it doesn't. Time for Plan B.

Plan B was that I should take up no space. I didn't defend myself against unfairness. Like any classic trying-to-take-up-no-space person, I was heroically passive aggressive. Had I had access to emojis back then, I'm sure I would have used them by the truckload in an effort to create for myself plausible deniability of the staggering levels of my toxicity.

"Fine" and "Whatever" became my endless refrains. But it's not fine. It's not whatever. Martyrdom to faith may be one thing, but martyrdom to self is never really a great spiritual plan. Your spirit prefers you to be a little bit more of a fighter than that. Like any journey, I discovered that Plan B is 360 degrees from Plan A, but no more useful. After all, 360 degrees from crazy is still crazy. There's a great song by the country band, SHeDAISY called "Mine All Mine" that begins:

> *Sun kisses the windowsill*
> *and I am still*
> *on my second cup of pity me.*

In short, I was being a martyr. Not speaking my truth clearly. To this day, there are threads of that still out there—the things I let people believe without defending myself, the things I never insisted upon correcting. They sideswipe me in certain company, and I am reminded of who I once allowed myself to be. And there's life in that too. That's good stuff as much as it's not. Amantine Lucile Aurore Dupin, a French novelist and memoirist best known by her pen name "George Sand," once wrote, "You will find no more thorough prude than someone who has some little secret to hide." The goal for a better version of life, or of self, is not to cover it up. The most miserable among us are the people trying to do this.

You live with who you used to be every bit as much as you live with who you are today. You can't erase it, but you can learn to live beyond it. Grief. Tragedy. Missteps. Wrong turns. These things don't go away. They don't get refilled. You can't get rid of them. They are a part of you. They have changed you. But what you can do is put life between you and the past. Perhaps a better one.

Over time, I began to learn a lot about myself on this journey to Stage Three. And I'll save you the suspense—even well over seven years later—I'm probably still a Two. But the journey is ever afoot, and I have learned a few things.

Maggie and I were sitting at lunch the other day, talking about a possibility in my life. It would involve working with low-income families to some extent. I shared with her my thoughts and my concerns, my misgivings and heartbreaks. At the end of the conversation, we got up to wash our plates in the sink and clean up. While I was wiping down the kitchen table, I asked her, "What do you think?"

She didn't even pause, as if the answer was obvious the whole time. She said, "I think you should do it. I think God has opened a door to something you've always wanted to do and you're good at doing. It may be hard on your heart, but you have a big enough heart to share."

And I thought to myself, *Three? Maybe never. But if this girl can go to bat for me, I might be able to pull off a Two-and-a-half.*

28.

where there's a will

You know, I don't talk about my son Will very much in my writing these days. He's in college, gone most of the time, and we don't have quite as many interactions. Certainly not as many in the present as Maggie and me. I'm not sure we did even when he was Maggie's age. He was always the quieter of the two, and I've always been very protective of him. Will doesn't seek interaction. You could always be confident that if he was interacting with you, it was because he wanted to. There is no falseness in him. No ability or desire to fabricate a moment that he doesn't care to be a part of.

In addition, he's twenty-one. Practically an old man! He has an actual life to navigate these days. One that could possibly be affected any time I choose to put pen to paper, and I don't want that for him. I just don't feel like I have that right. So I, for the most part, leave him to his privacy.

But, then there are times. Times like this morning when his "him"-ness, his essential "self"-ness, sends a frisson of love down my spine and it becomes imperative that I share. It's in the silliest things, really. The note he leaves on the counter written in the sharp scrawl that he's always had. The letters crafted, as I know from watching him over the years, like an artist: from bottom to top. The times he writes "Have a good day!" Then crosses out "good" and writes above it "great." What sweet intention went into that decision.

This morning, it was something so tiny. So unremarkable. But, still. The love I feel when I see it squeezes my heart. Love can be found most frequently in trivial things, right? Anyway . . . for some reason, Will is a sucker for the free sample table ladies at work. It is such a funny feature of the overlapping nature of life that when I was his age and became pregnant with him, I worked the free sample tables at my job. Maybe he is so patient and lovely with those ladies because he's attempting to support my career retroactively. Also, he's twenty-one. Free food is free food. But I think it's adorable that he buys the product. He doesn't just take advantage of the fact that it's free.

Nearly every morning that follows one of his closing shifts, I wake up to find a bag of his latest find in the pantry. He works at a health food market, so his finds are rather eclectic—a new flavor of gluten-free popcorn, dye-free chips. This morning, I woke to find a half-empty offering of apple-cinnamon fruit sticks. And he's not SO altruistic that he buys it for us—oh no, he buys it for himself. But it is such an endearing quality that he brings it home and places it exactly on the pantry shelf at eye level. Seeing it, I smile and know that when he wakes up, he will say to me, "You guys can have the rest. They're pretty good." An offering from a darling young man to the two women in his life.

I talk a lot with people about the comparative nature of things. I think many miseries begin with comparison. Comparing lives, incomes, expectations, experiences. So, I don't like to sound as if I am comparing the kids. I'm not. There is just no way to compare two such darling individuals.

While a comparison would be an insult to the charm of both, I think (I hope) you can acknowledge a contrast without slighting either of them.

In many ways, Maggie and Will are so very similar. They are generous and kind. Very clever. I think they are thankful beings. Lynn will tell you that they have two defining characteristics in common. One, their sense of humor. And two, "They love their mama."

But they diverge in many ways as well. I think all parents have an underlying awareness of the distinct characteristics of each of their children. Gifts that one child has that the other doesn't necessarily *not* have, but it may not be the gift that is most prominently on display. With respect to this idea, Will is the far gentler of my two children. Not that he feels things more than Maggie, or that she's a brute. And not that Will can't be sharp and abrupt, strong in word or deed. But his gentle nature is the characteristic of his most frequently on display.

I remember when his bunny, Oreo, died. Will was sleeping when I spotted Oreo's labored breathing out in the garden one morning. I came in and put a hand on Will's shoulder. He woke instantly, as we tend to do in the face of otherworldly matters.

"I think Oreo is dying," I whispered.

He sat up, awake before he was even awake, and we walked outside together. I started to follow him across the threshold of the sliding glass door, but he physically blocked me—like the old "mom seat belt" in a car. With his arm out. *Stop.*

"Stay here," he said, as if to mean, *He belongs to me. I will bear this first.*

I watched as he stepped through the gate, lowered to his haunches, and put his hand on Oreo's still form. He looked over at me and shook his head to indicate that Oreo was gone.

He looked back down at Oreo, smoothed his ears down for the last time, and said without looking at me, "Go get the shovel." When I asked if he wanted help, he declined.

"It's for me to do," he said, and I let him. He can be stubborn like that, an immovable force. When I say Will is gentle, I do not mean that he is fragile. I mean that he "does life" as it requires, and because of the fire that life baptized him in, he has grown a benevolent soul.

As I watch him grow into the man he is and will become, I am often astounded by his accomplishments. The sheer grit of him. He started so far from the finish line, and then spent years and years going in reverse. The story of his life is certainly not mine to tell, but high school was not pretty, and middle school was even worse.

I can recall praying one night so long ago. Meditating, really. Heartsick at the wall Will had built around himself that we could not breach. Watching Will, a little bit broken, lost and wandering. Suspended. Friendless. Alone. Unreachable. In the exhaustion of the moment and of this version of my life in progress, I sunk forward. Honestly, had you asked me at the time, I would have sworn the devil was trying to break me.

My forehead rested on the thread of the carpet in front of me, and my prayers ceased. Silence. And into Nothing, I began to speak as a mother would. No longer to pray, but to direct. To lay down my life.

"God," my heart spoke my desperate intention, "take me instead. Take my hope, and give it to Will. Take my courage, and give it to Will. Take my peace, and give it to him. Make me nothing. I will rebuild myself. Take everything I am, and give it to my son."

I don't know how long I lay folded over, prone, on the

carpet. I had been meditating for quite some time, and I was so exhausted in body and in spirit that I think I fell asleep a little. But I woke to the fleeting weight of what I perceived to be a hand on the crown of my head. I still feared seeing Mary, so I didn't move. But I smiled.

Nothing happened in an instant, of course. Nothing ever does. Miracles take some time. But looking back, I think He did just that. In the years that followed, I embarked upon a journey to believe in what I couldn't understand. It was like I couldn't make a single decision. Make sense of a single thing. A lot of wandering. A lot of amazing decisions and paths as well. I must give credit to those paths and to those people who met a rather chaotic me along the way and guided me to safety. But in so many ways, with regard to people and myself—I seemed to be relearning things I had at some point already known, but couldn't remember how to put in place. Everything was raw. Everything was scrambled and disordered. I was rebuilding from pieces of scrap metal that didn't fit.

But if you look at those same years for Will? In time, he possessed an extraordinary ability to endure, to have courage, and eventually, to thrive.

A few years into his journey, and on the advice of a friend, I signed Will up for the Putney School Summer Program, a creative arts program at a camp nestled in the Green Mountains of Vermont. We were on the Cape that summer, renting a cottage at the edge of an artists' colony in Dennisport. Tucked into a pocket of wild bamboo at the end of a rutted, gravel road, the cottage was built using reclaimed materials: timber from a former residence skirted the living room floor, bricks from an old sidewalk lined the patio. Repurposed stained glass formed the home's floor-to-ceiling bedroom windows, which opened, charmingly, like doors themselves. Pottery and books, shells and glass art decorated the home in a glittery, haphazard fashion which was as charming as it was dusty. You never knew what you were going to inherit as far as housing on the Cape from summer to summer. It was always a gamble. Always a wonder.

I was working at Brewster Day Camp still. Maggie was attending camp with me that summer, though Will had aged out of the program by then. One weekend, we drove four hours from Cape Cod to Putney, Vermont, to drop Will off at his first overnight camp experience. Three weeks. Three weeks, and a kid who had never been away from home.

I don't know what it is about the barometric pressure in Vermont, but as soon as we passed into the state, the peace flowed in. Will sat up—alert. Waiting. Watching. As soon as our dusty, travel-worn car crested the hill to find a working farm and open fields upon which the white New England dorms and wooden and glass art studios perched, Will was gone. I swear, if I could have just slowed down, he would have leapt out of the car and never looked back.

It was an experience that was transformative. He found that there was a place for his talents and personality in the world. In no small part, it made him. There were still hard times once we returned home. Of course there were. There are always bumps to be found on the road off into the sunset. But he returned home with a soul redefined.

Today, he stands at the precipice of a new adventure. One more year (plus a class or two or seven) in college. This September, he will study abroad in Japan. And those same feelings of watching him walk into kindergarten, or day camp, or middle school assault me at regular intervals. Will he be okay? Will he need me when I am so far away? Your babies are always your babies even when they are six feet tall.

I hold onto hope that it will be like his Putney experience: that if they can just slow the plane down enough on the runway, he will leap out into a new, extraordinary adventure. He, this boy of mine. This gentle soul who continues to shine in a million ways.

When I see him take the steps to make sure he has full-time hours this summer, to make sure he is studying for finals, to make sure he has gas in his car and an oil change on time . . . I am amazed that we've ever made it this far. How did we—who learned so much of life together—make it all work?

I frequently joke that Will "allowed me to raise him" because I had no idea what I was doing and he was always such an old soul that he seemed older than me even when he was very young. Plus, I just never understood men. I was raised predominantly by women and surrounded by a lot of women in a very Irish, very matriarchal family. So for me to raise a son on my own was a little bit like a science experiment. He gets mad at me when I say anything derogatory about my haphazard mothering. He's very protective of me, for me. "You are a great mom," he will say, and I am humbled that he thinks so.

From time to time, Maggie gets ticked off that I make her (her words) go to our Parish School of Religion every week, and to Mass with me. She has tracked the progression of Will's life and realizes that he never went to PSR and very rarely attends Mass. And I always blow her off. Tell her not to worry about it. Different people need different things. Once, I took the high-handed route of telling her that—*if she wants to*—we could have a really, *really* long conversation about the things Will didn't have that she does. Things like: lots of new clothes; a mother who was present, who wasn't working and going to night school; two parents for her whole life; summer camp on Cape Cod every summer since she was three years old; etc. She very quickly un-chose that conversation, as well she should have.

But the thing I never really say, maybe because I barely even have the words for it now, is that leading up to and during all of Will's hard times, I was kind of trying to preach God and Jesus to him and kind of force the Kingdom down his throat. And that was the wrong direction. That's the right direction for a lot of people. But the flavor of it was quite well proven to be the wrong direction in his particular circumstances.

The night I put my forehead down and gave up my claim. The night I admitted I could not pull him out of this hell he was in. That night . . . and believe me, I know it sounds crazy . . . but that night, I think Jesus went into hell for me and got him out. And the humility I feel in the face of that gift was something I never wanted to overstep. The divinity in it was no place for me to trespass. From that point forward, I allowed Will to navigate the direction of his personal faith.

So when I experience his nourishing character when he makes me stay back from the sight of Oreo, when I see his determined courage as he lines up everything to get himself to Japan and back, and even when I open the pantry door and see the sweet food offering of dried apple-cinnamon sticks . . . I can't help but marvel at the person he is and continues to be.

And in the back of my mind, I never ever forget that he is on the side of the angels. And what a blessing he is to me.

29.

the loves of my life

There was a Saturday about a month back that found Maggie and me in the produce section of our local Walmart. It must have been raining, and our favorite produce stand was closed. Squabbling with Maggie about some aimless bit of nothing-in-particular, I turned and saw someone I knew. Someone I hadn't seen for a long, long time. It was a woman I went to high school with. Startled, and thrown unceremoniously back in time seeing her over the banana display, I blurted out her name.

Truthfully, I would have rather ignored her. Not because she's a bad person, but because I am. I wasn't very nice to her once upon a time, and seeing her brought back all the embarrassment of my once-perceived martyrdom that—believe me—I took for quite a ride.

When we do happen to be in company—which might equal a sum total of fifteen minutes over the past twenty-five years—I am always socially awkward in her presence. I laugh too loud, stumble over words. I don't know for sure, but I suspect I fawn over her a bit too much and then, feeling like a maniac, I usually abruptly end our conversations and exit stage left.

You see, in 2006, I self-published a book entitled *Faking*

Normal. In it, I was ridiculously childish and disdainful of her—a fact which she may well be blissfully unaware of—but I know. I know it of myself, and I have no idea how to apologize for something so stale, so over. Something on the other side of a lifetime ago, and yet it was an unkindness and an intrusion that I've also never forgiven myself for. But we, the two of us, have no moments that lend themselves to realness. An apology at a reunion is absurd, and over a fruit stand in the middle of a discount store is even more so. So we talked. I laughed way too much and might have knocked over a pomegranate. Maggie looked at me like I was a foreign being—and one she wasn't particularly proud to be associated with at the moment. Eventually fate released us—thank you, sweet baby Jesus—and Maggie and I walked around the corner.

"Who *was* that lady?!"

Dramatically I answered, "Oh, just the person who stole my boyfriend in high school."

Maggie, captivated by the idea that I might have ever had a youth—wild, misspent, stolen, or otherwise—said, "Really?!"

"No! Not really," I laughed. "All she's ever been guilty of is scooping up a really good guy who I wasn't very nice to."

Instantly, Maggie leaped to my defense, "You *are so* nice!"

I smiled. ". . . a different kind of nice." I put my arm around her, kissed her on the top of her head, and pointed her out of the moment and toward the frozen pizza.

Maggie has this burning and recent desire to believe that most relationships that begin in high school end in marriage. So she held me back even as I wanted to move on from the topic. "But . . . ?"

I opened the freezer door. "But what? Pepperoni or sausage?"

"Pepperoni. But . . . do you think you guys would have been together forever?"

I shut the freezer door. Clearly, she needed a little more handling here. I looked at her and could remember all the moments leading up to that first . . . that first anything. First kiss. First hand to hold. First love. First everything. I recall it being so daunting, so crazy that I would ever be expected to jump into life and become a part of these mysterious masses of people and couples and lovers who populate our commercials and our love stories and our planet. How does that work? What will my role be? And please, GOD, tell me I only have to learn it all once. Once. With the first one. Let me never break a heart, let me never feel the claws of jealousy, let my heart never be broken or confused or lonely. I remember thinking at her age, *Please, God, let me get it right the first time*. And—standing in the middle of the frozen food aisle—some part of her needed to believe that could be possible . . . and it could. But still.

"No," I answered her. "We wouldn't have. We would have had to be two completely different people."

She didn't love that. Nothing about it even remotely fit into her twelve-year-old reality. Where was this world where I wasn't "nice" enough? Who was this person who didn't love her mother as much as she did, who would have forgiven her anything? The confusion, the look on her face as she processed this. It would have been funny if it hadn't been so beautifully touching.

And—oh my gosh!—isn't there so much we have to watch our children learn? The uncomfortable awareness of people's failures, including our own. No longer are we magical. Soon we are people in our own right, filled with people in our own pasts that don't fit their innocent view of this "Mom" they have come to know. The mind boggles at what she will endure and learn in the coming years. The loss of innocence in so many ways, but in so many others, the birth of something infinitely more gorgeous and precious.

By the time the taco aisle rolled around, Maggie had rallied. "Well, I'm *glad* she scooped him up,"—this she said a little peevishly, truth be told—"because if not, Will and me wouldn't get to be your kids!"

Oh, bless her! What sweet defense. I hugged her close . . . right there in the middle of shopping. Then I looked right at her lovely girl-woman face and said, "You want to know what I think?"

"What?" A petulant child, still irate in defense of her mother.

"I think you and me and Will? *We* were the ones who were meant to be. You two are the loves of my life."

She smiled.

"And I wouldn't trade that for anything in the world."

30.

the long way around

There is a change afoot. A little vein of gold ore has rippled through our lives and altered the status quo, brightening everything in its path. It is a change amid many changes and, as I am wont to do, I try to place it perfectly. To make it fit without changing anything else. To order things as I think they might be pleasing to everyone. Myself included.

But life isn't like that. The universe doesn't filter blessings through a funnel and into the only space they might fit. The universe doesn't see the order and go to the back of the line. No, the universe drizzles blessings over life in a dizzy, sort of haphazard and celebratory fashion. Our only job is to turn the umbrella upside down and collect as many drops as possible.

And in some ways . . .

Well, in a lot of ways, I feel like I put my needs in front of the kids' their whole lives. Will's more so than Maggie's. That's my knee-jerk self-narrative. That I've been a taker and not a giver. But when I really study my life over the past seven years, I think that's actually not the case at all. For seven years, I have sacrificed anything I might call my own—gladly and willingly—to be of service to these two. To right my wrongs.

To be a port in the storm. To be the calm amid chaos. And it was a choice I made 100% peacefully. It was a pure pleasure to be of use. To be of service.

I devoted my life to myself as well. My own heart. My own soul. And, in many ways, my own pain. I sat many nights in the dark untangling my own secret shames. Going back to where it broke and healing it properly. I said to a friend once that I feel like everywhere I look, there are broken pieces. She rephrased my words more gently. "Only frayed edges," she said. "And you can tie them back together."

My life was solitary. It did not look like other people's lives. It did not look like every holiday special. It did not look like Valentine's Day commercials. It was not reflected back to me by the media or by Hollywood as any version of success or completeness. But I knew that this was right. I knew that this was the journey I understood: to be of service. This, the long road. The long way around.

I purged my broken dreams. I made peace with lost paths. Rejected comparative thinking. I built up a world that was my definition of success, that was complete to my way of thinking. I devoted myself to the only two things I ever wanted to do well: be a good person and be a good mother.

Along the way, I hope I was a good friend. Undoubtedly I was a good colleague. And I hope I was faithful. I think I was. I kept my head down and worked to be patient. I was determined to be a channel of peace. I worked to meet chaos with gentleness in so many places, and I think I succeeded as much as I didn't at that. But I wanted so much, and it was so clear to me that I should try to clear out confusion and make a little light.

But, these blessings. *Drip drop*. They came when I wasn't

looking. Here and there. A little of this. A little of that. A blink. A smile. A wish. *Drip, drip, drop.*

I said to Maggie the other day, "Is this okay? Is this weird? Are we okay in this new space? On the doorstep of this new thing?"

She unfolded herself from her bed and came over and gave me a hug.

"Mom," she said. "You have given your life to us. There isn't a time I remember where you took anything for yourself. Not food. Not money. Not clothes. Not time."

She said, "Heck . . . I had to force you to promise me the other day that you would use that Kohl's Cash on yourself and not me and Will!" And we laughed for a little bit at that. Then her expression sobered.

"Mom," she said again. "It's time. It's time for you to take something for yourself. Something that is just for you. It's okay—*we're okay*—because of you."

And so.

And so we are. And so I will.

"Do not come any closer," God said. "Take off your sandals,
for the place where you are standing is holy ground."
~ Exodus 3:11

~ Witness, January 2013

One summer evening, I walked down to the kitchen, and Misa was alone there.

"Tea, Monamudd?" she asked. She always runs both my first and last name together like it is one long word. I took her up on it and then sat at the counter and confessed a bit of my ongoing struggle to her. The guilt that wouldn't leave me. This train wreck of a thing with John. All the unforgiveness that would never come.

After listening, she said to me, "You know, you can just walk away from 'crazy.' You don't even have to tell it you're leaving."

"You don't have to figure it out," she went on. "You don't need to beat yourself up about why you did what you did, or didn't do what you didn't do. Just put it down and walk away from it. One day, you'll turn around and realize that you have forgiven him his crazy. You've forgiven yourself your humanity. But for now? Just be in this kitchen. On a rainy night, with a cup of tea, and someone who loves you."

It took me a long time to get past this. I'm not going to lie. I wasn't able to just simply put it down. But what I was able to do was open my eyes to the rest of it. The purity of a storm night. The cup of tea. The people who love me. If I would have let it, that *summer would have crippled me—wrapped up as it was in many, many issues: my fears, the divorce, my guilt, my own unhealed wounds past and present. All told, about 3% of it was actually the part that John brought to my door. As I was able to peel back the layers of it, I found that it was an amalgamation of so many layers of loss, coming at a time in my life when I was finally capable of acknowledging loss. So it all sort of came flooding in on the tail feathers of this one single event.*

I could see that in two years, John's presence in my life would be whittled down to two sentences, if any at all: "That was the summer I met John. He was pretty crazy." And so if John was going to get two sentences, then didn't everything else around me—all of the wonderful things and people—deserve their sentences too?

I learned to kayak that summer. I can still hear the echo of Misa's dad, an old Navy man, hollering instructions from the shoreline on those chilly Cape Cod mornings. I went to Provincetown and got a tattoo on my back. It says one word: "Believe." Believe in what? Anything. *Anything bigger than yourself.*

My friend Rob and I went to a play at the Monomoy Theatre in Chatham. The kids and I played hooky from camp one afternoon. I took them mini-golfing and to the Brewster Scoop for ice cream. We ate dinner on the beach. I made videos of our time there and sent them home to Mom. I made sure I wrote in my journal all the things I loved about the day. Every day.

Like God said to Moses—and Misa pointed out to me in her way—"Stop. Take your shoes off. You are already on holy ground."

I attended church at St. Joan of Arc every Sunday. There was a song the cantor would sing directly after Communion when we were all seated before the Concluding Rites of Mass. Its words are from the Gospel of Matthew: "Come to me, all you weary. Come to me and find strength." And I was weary. I couldn't remember not being weary. One Saturday evening, I decided to go to confession. I confessed my guilt over my divorce—my two divorces—and all of the pain I had caused in the lives of so many, especially my children. I had no idea how to do the mechanics of confession anymore, it had been so long. I'm not sure it mattered, as I couldn't seem to do anything but cry. Finally, the priest interrupted my crying—

"Ma'am?" he said.

Then louder, when I didn't stop. "MA'AM!"

I looked up at his shadow through the screen. He said, "I don't think Jesus wants you to be so sad. What He wants is for you to be here. And here you are! You are forgiven. Of course you are forgiven. You need never have worried otherwise."

One night that summer, I was meditating in my bedroom. My bedroom in the house was an old, dormered, third-story room which overlooked the rooftop skylights of the single-storied kitchen wing of the house out my window below. But I always meditated facing the twin windows that overlooked the back of the house. These looked out over the tops of the ash and cedar trees that surrounded a dormant pond, a sight I found peaceful, somehow beautiful in its humble sacrifice to the passage of time.

Gently into one moment of my meditation drifted the lyrics to an old prayer, The Prayer of St. Francis, one whose words create the lyrics to the beloved song "Make Me a Channel of Your Peace." The whole song is a treasure, but the part that drifted toward me was one specific part:

"O, Master, grant that I may never seek
So much to be consoled as to console;

To be understood as to understand;
To be loved as to love with all my soul."

And for the first time in a long time, I felt something open in my heart, somewhere deep down where joy lives. It seemed to be the answer I was searching for, though I have no idea why it came unbidden the way it did. It is in pardoning that we are pardoned.

It hit me in that moment that I had been loving in the wrong direction all my life. Creating all sorts of storms and catastrophes in relationships and insisting that love still rain down on me without giving anything of myself on its behalf. Judy once said to me, "The one who loves less *has all the power in the relationship. You have set yourself up as the one who loves* less *your entire adult life."*

On the wings of these lyrics came the realization that I needed to change that. I needed to learn to understand. I needed to console. I needed to forgive. I needed to love, and I mean really, really *love someone. Finally, with a great exhale of the spirit, I accepted that that might take time. That I, too, would come to learn the humility of time's passing.*

The prayer goes on to say:

"Where there's despair in life, let me bring hope,
Where there is injury, Your pardon,
And where there's doubt, true faith in you."

And suddenly. Quietly. I had the sense that I could do that in my life. While I was waiting, while I was learning the stillness of grace, the humility of time—I could do that. Without even changing a single thing. Life doesn't always have to be great waves of emotion and energy and change. At times, it is only moment to moment, knitting together every moment you are in. Trying—just trying—to be a channel of peace. As my friend, Jenny, wrote on her Blessings & Raindrops *blog one day:*

"I don't want to miss the life God has for me. I want to do the one thing before me and trust God for what will come tomorrow. And then, I want to do that thing and trust God for the next one. And again, and again, and again."

Someone once told me that God doesn't get tired of forgiving. He is always ready with his mercy, just as we are with our own children. It is we who get embarrassed and tired of asking. I think certainly that God is a perfect example of selfless love. While I believe He has the desire to be known, He lacks the ego that requires it. His goal is selfless: It is that you feel loved—not even that you acknowledge that it is Him loving you.

If it makes you feel more comfortable to call Him "the Universe," then fine. Call Him that. If His love gets from Him to you in a book. In an idea. In a song. In a poem. Wonderful.

If you are too busy and He can only touch your heart at sunset, then He'll take it. As long as you feel it. As long as you know you are loved.

I think God knew that I wasn't able to process a father's love. Not that it wasn't given to me. Not that I wasn't loved. I was. I am. By my stepdad, by my beloved grandpa, and by my own father. I was loved, but I couldn't process a Father's love in quite the same endless way that I could process a Mother's love. And so, to love me, He sent his mother.

I was raised in St. Mary's Parish, and through her I learned faith. He sent His protection through my aunt Katie. He sent

His strength through my grandma. He sent His companionship through Lynn, who saved me as a child. He held my hand through Misa, who saved me as an adult. Through Cathy, who in her darkest hour was still given the grace to be God's voice to me in mine. Through Shelley, who entered my world and showed me a wonderful new one. Through Marcia, who gave me safe harbor every time I was lost. Through Judy, who showed me the way to free my heart, and through my own mother, who has never not been there. She has always been the love of my life. I have found a home at the Assumption of the Blessed Virgin Mary Parish where I am a teacher and parishioner.

I have been blessed. I learned God's love through the love of all the mothers He has placed on my path, and through His grace, I have become one of them. God continues to show me His love through the joy I receive in being a mother to so many. To my own children and to the students who have blessed my life through the years.

A long time ago, I was listening to a show on NPR on which the speaker was discussing Paul McCartney's writing of the Beatles' song, "Let it Be." He said that what many people don't know is that Paul McCartney was writing about his own mother. He was struggling with life, and in one of his fitful bouts of sleep, he dreamed of his mother, who had died of breast cancer when he was very young. He woke up feeling restored and comforted.

But what is music but our modern-day poetry? And, like poetry, music speaks a universal human language. It has the power to comfort in any way we, as listeners, need it to do so. Even now when I am facing struggles in life, the knots that I cannot untangle, I will hear it. Inevitably, curiously, unfailingly, I will hear an old voice on any nearby radio. In the car. At the gas station pump. Over the department store speaker:

"When I find myself in times of trouble, Mother Mary comes to me . . ."

And I know all over again that I am not alone. That there will be an answer.

CHAPTER FIVE

2018

"Autobiography in Five Short Chapters"
by Portia Nelson

Chapter Five

I walk down another street.

31.

the queen of swords

The Winter House soaps. These are products we make in our family company, and they are divine. Some are sweet. Some spicy. Some citrus and herbaceous. Full disclosure: they are made by a man we know and not Maggie herself. She enjoyed the process for the longest time . . . but lye, it is an unkind substance, and soon she was ready to move onto her first love: facial care.

But before she could move on entirely, she needed a willing soul to take over production. And who did she choose, you may ask? Well, you see, six months ago, I met a boy. Well, I met the boy twenty-nine years ago. I met the man six months ago.

To my middle school class, I am reading a book called *Walk Two Moons*. In the book, the main character, Salamanca, is telling her grandparents a story. She muses that to tell her story, she has to tell the story of a girl named Phoebe because, she says, "Just as the brick was behind the plaster wall, my story is behind Phoebe's." So to tell her story, she has to tell them Phoebe's story.

It is the same with the Winter House soaps. The story of how these soaps came to be rests behind a story that started a long time ago. My mom has a great, giant wooden sign hanging on her kitchen wall which says, "What is meant to be has already begun." So it is with our story. This partnership, which debuted only recently, actually began decades ago.

I met Dan during our freshman year of high school. Our relative roles were pretty stereotypical at the time. He sat behind me in French class and was a little bit of a troublemaker. To be honest, even though "troublemaker" wasn't my assigned high school role, it was easy to do in this class. Our French teacher was an unfortunate woman. God bless her, but she was a woman on the edge. Dan frequently got himself kicked out of class, and I had to walk him to the office.

"Monique!" she would bark in class. "Take Daniel to the principal!" And we would get up and leave the room together.

That's about all we did was leave the room together. To my knowledge, I don't think we ever made it to the office. It is more accurate to say that I simply walked *with* him out the door of French class. From there, we went our separate ways. He went . . . wherever. I used my "Get Out of Jail Free" card in my own way as well. Hey, I was a cheerleader—I couldn't make trouble. But there was no law stating I couldn't capitalize on somebody else's.

Dan and I occupied different strata in school. He was occupied with his chosen role, and so was I. The only time the two roles existed side by side was during this class, or any time I caught his attention in the hallway. For my part, he was way out of my league. Wilder than I was, or would have ever been comfortable being, and (he will hate this being in print) *painfully* good-looking. *My eyes!!*—that kind of good-looking. Nature had heaped an unreasonable amount of attractiveness on him, even at a young age. It was ridiculous and, to me, intimidating.

I tried to keep most of our conversations brief because I was actually rather tongue-tied around him, but he pulled me in a lot.

Teasing me. Doing things to get my attention. These moments I remember again only because he has reminded me of them. I confess, I didn't really carry the memories with me over time. But, teasing aside, he was kind. He was always so nice to me.

It was his kindness that led me back to him and his kindness, again, which led to Dan joining our little household endeavor. You see, when we first met back up again, Dan said that he had always wanted to learn how to make soap. Remembering his kindness, I thought he was just being indulgent. And having no small amount of ego to call my own, I also thought he was just trying to get my attention.

I said to Mags, "Dan says he wants to learn how to make soap." She laughed, and I might have used air quotes. A month later, I had to retrench. "Okay, no, seriously. He actually does want to learn how to make soap." So, one rainy afternoon, Maggie taught him how—and a partner was born. My road to him, and this, and us, and all things Winter House has been a long one. Long and winding. But ever-fruitful. Ever divine.

Years and years ago, I found myself on vacation on Cape Cod alone. The story of why is as simple as it is complicated and not really the focus at this point. But on this trip, I was solitary—yes, lonely—and seeking. Seeking what? I wasn't sure. I was closed off from my family at the time and some of my friends. Closed off from myself a fair bit as well.

In my wanderings, I stumbled upon a woman who was a "seer" of sorts. This was not her job, per se. She was giving me a facial one afternoon. But when she said she could "see" things about people, I believed her. For three reasons. One: I believe that the Spirit can be in other people, and they meet you on the road and set truth down in front of you. Two: I believe that you can sense it—truth—when it is given. And I believe it gives you strength for the journey. The third reason I believed her was strictly pragmatic. I believed her because she was not charging me any money, and she wasn't wrapped in scarves and trying to sell me tarot cards.

As I was lying in our lemon- and rosemary-scented steamy room, she announced, "The Queen of Swords."

I peeled open my eyes. "What?"

"I'm sorry," she said. "It hit me as soon as you walked through the door. You have a potent spirit, did you know that?"

I didn't. My spirit, in fact, was at a relatively low ebb at the time, and I told her so.

She repeated, "The Queen of Swords. That's you."

"What does that mean?" I asked.

She stopped working on my face, shrugged—a half-hearted little motion she didn't really commit to—then went back to her task. "You have many battles in front of you . . ." she divulged after a time.

Battles?! I wanted to leap up and ask a thousand questions. What kinds of battles? Health battles? Personal battles? *Actual* battles? But her spirit was so calm and I was so comfortable that I stayed prone on the massage table.

"Will I win them?" I asked. It seemed the only question of value at the moment.

Peaceful and easy, she smiled. "You'll be strong enough for them."

Fifteen minutes later, somewhere in the middle of a mud mask, she spoke again.

"Do you think you will ever get married again?"

I laughed. "No."

Love had done me wrong. Or maybe I had done it wrong? Isn't the truth always somewhere in the middle of all that mess? So I said no. No, I don't want love. No, I don't want the bother. But what I meant was: No, I won't risk it. No, my heart is tired. No, I have lost my desire. No, I no longer believe I am capable.

She made a bit of a noncommittal sound and then added, "You will again. After all the work is done." Which was a fine thing to say, but she didn't really know me. I closed my eyes, and she didn't say anything more on the subject until I was leaving.

"About before?" she began, and I thought, *This is it. This is where she is going to sell me tarot cards or her mind-reading services.* I wasn't angry. Just a little dismissive. Of course. Of course there would be a cost. I turned around as I was pulling on my gloves. It was winter at the time. Winter on Cape Cod.

She smiled a smile that, for one moment, engaged my lost sense of hope. A smile that made me think, maybe, she could see me. She could read my tired mind and my exhausted heart. A smile that made me wonder if I would come back to myself one day and wouldn't always be this rather diminished version.

She said, ". . . I think it will surprise you who it is."

I tried to get her to clarify. "Is it somebody I already know?"

She smiled again, a vague little shadow. "It will be someone who was there all along, you just didn't see him at first." Which, I think we can all agree, didn't really answer my question. But in time, I began to see that it did something even better.

And maybe I was a fool. And maybe she was a hack. Maybe she was greedy. Maybe she was a liar. That is the beauty of the Spirit. That He can use the best of what you can be, rather than who you are. He can use the best of you to impart peace, to be of service. To bless another with a message. To keep a spark glowing in even the darkest of times.

And maybe it sounds crazy now. To hear it, it sounded crazy. To believe it, even more so. But at that moment, she was Truth to me. I believe you know *truth*, the big Truth—Capital T, Truth—when you hear it, if you are willing to listen.

When I was down, I remembered this Capital T, Truth. That this person was not far from me. When I was lonely, when people worried about me that I was only looking back and not moving forward, this Capital T, Truth sustained me. It held its truth in silence. When I encountered all of the battles that were before me, I was at peace on that front. Yes, I was alone now, but I wouldn't be forever because I knew that road, that journey, would make its way back to me in time.

As the years went by, as battles were fought and won, as the calendar pages turned, I had the beauty of that one Truth. Yes, I was alone at the moment. Yes, I would learn to be solitary well. But my Truth told me that one day it wouldn't be the same. That one day it would change. One day.

Then one day, *one day* came. One day, the boy I remembered, and the man he had become, brought me a tool I needed to create a space in the basement for Maggie to make soap. I had been just fine completing this project on my own, but he brought me an electric sander which would make it go a lot faster.

And so. Twenty-five years after I had last seen him, I heard his car pull in the driveway. I opened my front door and stepped barefoot onto the porch.

"My hero!" I called, and he turned. "You've saved me!"

And he is. And he did.

32.

you don't get it

You don't get it.

You don't get it. An old phrase, maybe an old-fashioned taunt. *You don't get it* is something we've all heard applied to academics or emotions. In school yards. In arguments. In our prayers. *You don't get it.* To say you "get" something of course refers to understanding. You don't *understand* it.

Maggie got mad at me last night. Oh, she will point to some specific thing—her mad has grown layers and wings since we last spoke. She'll sit on it for a while, for sure. She'll stoke the fires for as long as she cares to. Her third-grade teacher used to tell me, "Maggie doesn't ever start the fight, but she doesn't ever let it end, either." And truer words have rarely ever been spoken.

What happened is essentially this: One friend of hers doesn't like another friend, and it bothers her. That's the concept boiled down to its essential parts. And Maggie wants to know why. She wants to understand *why* this one friend doesn't care for the other, but she is not being granted that information. Maggie believes she is entitled to that information, and has yet to learn that not every piece of information that passes her is her concern or her right. The answer to her fury (the injustice of it!) was a simple one, and one I told her repeatedly:

"Maybe you just don't get to know that information."

Maybe she just doesn't *get to know* that. She doesn't *get to know* the reason for the dislike—there could be a host of reasons why the information is not given to her, and they are all irrelevant. Her only working piece of information is in the single digits: *You don't get to know that.*

She was livid! Oh, did she spin around and around on that! She wants to help! She wants to be able to tell her friend so she can fix it! It's not fair! And in all of her arguments, my answer was one: "But. You just don't get to know." That much was as obvious to me as it was untenable to her.

And is her motivation pure? Surely it is, but maybe it isn't. But how many of us have lived through the varying shades of emotion that come with something we just don't "get" to understand. Something we just don't "get" to solve. The things you don't get are the hardest things to learn, are they not? If "getting it" is the beginning of understanding, then knowing what we "don't get" has got to be the beginning of wisdom.

One summer, I read a book by Alice Koller entitled *An Unknown Woman*. In it, the main character was on a journey to personal fulfillment, and one of her perceived steps along this path was to try to right her wrongs, to apologize for the hurts she had caused people in the past. She began to find these people and apologize to them, and it was a rough road, one rather thwarted by circumstance and disconcerting to both her and the reader.

Whatever peace she had hoped to attain remained steadily out of reach. People were confused by her intrusion. Startled by her presence out of the past and into their present lives, on the phone, in a letter, at their cocktail parties. She spun around in her mind a little bit on that. *Why did these people seem not to get her purpose?* Maybe she had not been clear enough in her apology. Maybe she needed to explain some more.

By the middle of the book, she finally arrived at this madly uncomfortable revelation that it wasn't that they didn't *get* it ... it was that they *didn't need it.* Her effect on their lives rippled on in her mind, yes, but not in theirs. Her pop-up tornado appearances in people's lives only served her own ego. It was at that point that she realized a truth she had to accept: that her rather inflated sense of self-importance led her to believe this exercise was a necessary one, but it wasn't. And it was at that point where her journey actually began.

How often do we deem our wants to be other people's needs? When I look back on my life, I see it, and it is unsettling. It is hard work to accept one of the incontrovertible facts of life—some things you don't *get* to have. Some past mistakes don't lend themselves to forgiveness. Some breakdowns, eruptions, and missed healings you just have to keep, whether by circumstance or fate, even in all their uncomfortable and unruly forms. They fit nowhere, like a piece of furniture out of place that you can't give away. We learn that we don't *get* to be understood. Maybe we don't *get* to help. Like the woman in the book, maybe we don't *get* to have a narrative that forgives us. Some things in life are just like that.

You don't get to soften the edges.

You don't get to smooth the sheets.

You just don't *get* it.

How can I explain to Maggie the number of times in relationships she won't get the last call? We don't get the final act, the last word, the encore performance? Times she will have to release a feeling or a situation or a person back into the wild without the benefit of an apology, an explanation, or our feelings protected. To me, it calls to mind what it would be like to release a jellyfish back into the ocean: flailing, all-over tentacles, the damage they inflict out of fear. Even as you try to help, you get stung by needles in every direction; the mark they leave behind tends to linger.

BUT. If you can do the work to accept the reality of what you *don't get*, you do receive the impeccable gift of what you do get: You do get the calm of knowing that there isn't a thing that can't wait the span of a day. You do get the peace of understanding where you end and—blessedly, thank you God—where the work of another begins. You get the grace of the kind of wisdom that knows it's not a barb, but rather the deepest comfort to hear a friend say, "What you need to remember is that this isn't about you."

How true that can be! What a wonderful blessing when you can detach any ego from the choices around you and release them, not in an angry stomp of "taking my toys and going home" way, but in such a way that you can place something from the palm of your hand into the water and release it downstream. A way that forgives without expectation, that releases without fear, that blesses without judgment.

And as for my sweet daughter who has turned bitter on me? Well, for her recall a few bits of wisdom that I have learned along the way:

—That a good idea right now will still be a good idea in twenty-four hours.

—That there isn't a conversation that isn't made softer after time.

—That there isn't a love on earth that hasn't had to learn the grace of patience.

After she had stomped upstairs last night, I turned to Dan and said, "Tell me she'll like me again someday."

He laughed, a little rumble I love so much, and said, "She will someday. Probably tomorrow. The day after that? I couldn't say."

I paused at the wisdom of one who has raised a teenage daughter before me, then accepted it: I don't *get* to have her like me today.

I smiled at him, then went back to my reading. "Fair enough."

33.

a nana moment

One of the greatest things about my mom is her ability to sell a joke. To wait just long enough after the delivery for the hearer to suffer in faint horror, but not long enough to suffer for long. Who can forget when a grade school friend of mine, for some odd reason, said something vaguely mocking about Australians. Mom, with a completely straight face, said, "Ramona's father is Australian." Let me save you the time it takes to ask the question—that is not true. But she loves to tip a moment on its ear and, so too, a short-sighted belief system.

Or the time I walked into the kitchen to find her cutting an article out of *Dear Abby*, lost in a fit of giggles. I asked her what she was doing, and she replied that the article was written by a woman who claimed to be "attracted to her daughter's boyfriend."

When my college boyfriend came to pick me up for our date that evening, she said, "Look, Dave! They published my letter!" I mean . . . the horror as we watched him read it. The hilarity. She swatted him on the back about halfway through the letter.

"Ah, I'm just kidding you!" she said, all spiky hair and ribald laughter.

This Christmas, I told her that Dan needed a belt that fit. "A good belt," I said, and she said my stepdad, Bill, was on it. He insisted that he be the one to give Dan this gift.

A few weeks later, she and I were talking, and I realized that when I had said "a good belt" and when mom had said "a good belt," we knew we meant a *sturdy* belt. A belt for a man who makes tables and works with power tools all day. She expressed concern that Bill didn't quite get the memo on that, and she was going to ask him to return his purchase.

I didn't want him to feel bad, so I said, "Well, maybe it will be okay! I don't want him to be sad!"

She said, "No. It's all wrong. He needs to return it."

I said, "Well, maybe he could use it anyway?"

She said, "No. He needs to return it."

I said, "But . . . what does it look like?"

She waited. Then she blurted it out on a wave of drama. "*Oh, Ramona!*" she said. *"He's going to hate it!* It has a GIGANTIC belt buckle made out of wood and etched into the buckle is Santa Claus kneeling at the *manger*!"

"*What?!?!*" I was shocked. Horrified, and no longer caring about Bill or his *stupid* feelings—what a ridiculous purchase! I said, "There is NO WAY IN HELL Dan would be caught DEAD in that! Return it!!"

And then she laughed. Laughed, and laughed, and laughed.

"I'm kidding! Bill just got him a dressy belt, which is not what you meant," she said, laughter still punctuating every breath of the sentence. Then she went on, "Bill is standing here looking at me like I'm a maniac. I thought of it last week—I've been waiting *forever* for the perfect opportunity to say it!"

She said, "I told Bill, 'Ramona is going to think this is hilarious!', but he didn't believe me."

"*Tell him he's right!*" I yelled at her. "I think it's *horrible!* You almost gave me a heart attack!"

"I knew you'd love it!" she said. And she's right, I do. I told Mags about it the other day at dinner and could barely get it out because I was laughing so hard.

Last night, in a blink, I had a Nana moment. While explaining to Dan the nuts and bolts of the retreat Maggie was attending this weekend, he had quite a few questions.

"So it's at Assumption?" he asked. I said yes.

"They sleep at the church?" he asked. "Is it like a lock-in?"

I said, "No. They are at the church and the school and the parish center, but at night they leave and go to Sleep Houses." These are parents who are willing to house six to eight teenagers overnight both Friday and Saturday. Angels on this earth, if you ask me.

I explained this all to Dan and then said, "Oh. Did I not tell you I'm having eight teenagers spend the night here both nights this weekend?"

I relayed this story to Mags while on our way to the retreat. I said, "And it would have been amazing if I hadn't started laughing halfway through, and he knew immediately that those were NOT my plans for myself or my house."

Mags said, "Of course you started laughing . . ."

I said, "I know, it hit me right in the silly. How can you not laugh? I don't know how Nana does it . . ."

The ride was silent. We sat at one stoplight, then another.

Mags said, "Nana will still think it's hilarious . . ."

I said, "She totally will."

Then she said, "But Nana would have sold that better."

And I agreed. "Oh, she absolutely would have. She would have killed it."

34.

only the young

Will. My sweet Will has returned from Japan. And as he knew in theory, and I knew in practice, he has returned not the same. What has always been a square peg in a round hole is now a brick through the eye of a needle. It is a test of endurance, no? Everyone wants to see the finish line. But we forget the joy that can be found in not yet being in sight of it. There's an impatience, a frustration, in seeing what's on the horizon and not being able to get there fast enough.

And so I remind him that time will get him there, and he reminds me that he knows. I remind him that he must arrive at that platform with tickets in hand—tickets being a degree, experience, etc. Arriving well is always better than arriving fast.

But, oh I know where he is. As my mother once said to me, "I have been where you are, and if I could take this from you, I would." Oh, I have been so ready to go. Oh, I have had a fire at my feet and home in the rearview. *Highway run.*

"Mom," he said to me, "if I could leave tomorrow, I would." And I know this to be true. It is only his trust in the promises he made himself that steady the twitching reins.

". . . but I know," he added, "I will never forgive myself

if I don't leave with the degree I promised myself." I agree, and recite to him the advice of my old friend Charlotte Brontë in *Jane Eyre*, that you must keep the promises you made to yourself when you were sane because they are the only guideposts you have when you are feeling the insanity of impatience and passion.

I remember being where he is. Not at his age . . . no. I was much older when the ties that bound began to chafe. And in response to that, I pushed. I tried to make room within my ties for the expansion of me. For the parts of that I did well, I am proud. And for the parts that I didn't, I have mourned.

But in the meantime, I tell him to make plans. Make connections. Research. See. Search. He plans. He waits. Nevertheless, he persists. As he should. As youth will.

I love young people because they have so much in them. They have the juice that is required to push a generation forward, and they need to. That is their job while they are young, just as it was ours when we were.

There is an arrogance to youth that is necessary—pushing forward, starting a life—these things require a certain willingness to fly blind. A certain recklessness, a certain speed. And of course every generation thinks they invented life—but that's the arrogance they need to leap. I say leave them to it. We are the wind under the wings at this point, as one friend of mine would say. We are the soil, rather than the stem.

And Maggie, I see her behind Will. Oh how she impatiently waits her turn. She gnaws at the reins. She bumps up against the barn door that is us telling her to wait her turn. She and her friends practice being grown-ups in the way they believe they know. Learning how to navigate boys, and authority, and other girls. They can't wait for high school, and college, and she already knows which girls she's going to have an apartment with when she is older . . . and the make-up and the bras and the short shorts. And the *this* . . . and the *that*. It's not new. None of it is. In a classic twist of irony, youth is never new.

Sure, in some significant ways, the world has changed. But in so many ways, the world is as old as time. It's all the same as it ever was. They stand poised, waiting for their turn. *A generation waits for dawn.*

A few weeks back, we went to a restaurant called Hendel's in Florissant, Missouri, for the occasion of Dan's mom's birthday. On the way there, Dan showed me his grandmother's old house on the corner of two streets in Old Town Florissant. It's so funny to look back at what he shows me of his younger life. *Seems like yesterday, but it was long ago.* I marvel that, for a brief moment, our timelines overlapped and I was right there. *Right there,* and I knew none of him.

At one point at dinner, while we were talking to Dan's daughter and son-in-law, the conversation landed on someone we both knew. I said the name of this long-ago memory of a person, and Dan, surprised, repeated it.

He looked at me. "You knew him?"

I said, "Of course I knew him. I worked the front counter at a pizza place. Although, to be honest, we didn't talk much unless he needed 100 hot wings at 1 A.M . . ." and we both laughed.

Then just for a second, Dan and I walked backwards in time together. There are moments when, as the old Eagles lyrics go, "out of the silver light the past comes softly calling." And those moments are enjoyable to dip a toe back into from time to time.

"Who was his friend?" I asked. "Remember? He never really talked . . . ?"

Dan supplied it, and I said, "Was *that* his name?"

"Yep." He smiled.

"Huh. I never knew it. Seemed best to not know, plausible deniability and all that . . ." and we laughed again.

I look at couples who are lucky enough to have found each other young, and in a way, I envy them. I envy them in the same vague way I envy those who found their lives young, their purpose young. Will, with such focus at such a young age. Maggie, with her dreams of a soap business. Instead, I was on a path that set fires and beat at the bushes. *Against the wind.* And I tend to think Dan chose that path as well.

But we fast-forward. Life has carved in us the journey we've made. And there I sat that night, incredibly grateful that the very life I insisted on rattling and setting on fire eventually poured me out exactly where I started—there, in that restaurant, next to a man I barely grazed thirty years ago. *The joy of rediscovering you.* Life is a funny author.

You know, Maggie loves the comfort of Dan and me together, and to her it is attributed to a common youth. She's a little bit wrong because—although we knew a lot of the same people and places—we didn't really ever occupy the same space in our youth. But maybe she's a little bit right. There is a commonality in a shared youth experience, a foundation that only time can build. It is one of the few things in the world today that youth, speed, and innovation cannot produce. For all of its marvels, the modern world is still limited. It can't produce history, it can't create time. Dan and I get to have it simply because we get to. We had nothing to do with the overlap of our timelines; it was only a gift that managed to come back around. A gift that we met again after a very long road.

Yes, there is a perfect purpose for the movement, the passion, and the impatience of youth. There is a necessity to it. Will will move his path forward, and Maggie will take her part on after him. Time will move on, and today's youth will grow beyond, and another will take its place. And it will be. And it will be. And it will be again.

Youth is an Eagles song. A Bob Seger song. A Journey song. *Another night in any town.* Only the young.

But for me. For many. I hope for us all, there are always far more precious moments beyond youth. Moments you don't push life so much anymore. Moments you relax and pass the reins. Moments you sit inside the warm glow of an old hometown restaurant, remembering.

These are the moments for a little-too-tipsy dinner here and there. The moments for night moves, still. There are last-minute Friday night dinner dates. Spontaneous bonfires with the neighbors. Christmases and birthday parties. Falling asleep on the couch. Snowy mornings to sleep in. These, the no-longer-youth days, are a landing place, not a loss.

I love Max Ehrmann's line, "Surrender gracefully the things of youth" . . . and the more I live, the more I learn that a surrender it is, indeed. A blissful, sweet surrender that gives everything back kinder and softer. It is the release of knowing you have carried your part of the timeline forward, and that is enough.

35.

a resting place

One of the things I have had the hardest time accepting about myself, and sharing authentically with other people, is the fact that I am perfectly balanced. And before you think I mean that in a gloriously flattering light . . . let me explain.

Years ago, I was having an internal struggle to understand a person who had surprised me very much with a darker side. And through my discoveries, I finally had to admit something that I never quite wanted to recognize: the universe is a perfect balance. And that can be a beautiful thing, indeed. But we can't only operate on the side that is gorgeous. If we know that, we have to acknowledge that where there exists one, there also exists an equal opposite. Beauty and light, darkness and grotesque. They balance each other. And we, with the universe both outside and within, we are perfect little balances unto ourselves. My realization was that if indeed this person shone so brightly, then I was naïve not to expect an equal and perfectly balanced capacity to operate in the opposite direction. He wasn't a bad human being, but he operated within a range that was a bit too wide for me. A range that, ultimately, I chose not to be a part of.

I had a friend once traveling through menopause. She was alarmed by the intensity of her feelings and reactions at first, but eventually settled into a grudging acceptance of the process. She said that a very wise woman had explained to her, "A person who is very low-key might have the joy of a low-key experience. But you are not. You are bright. You swing wide. You are larger than life. So it stands to reason that you are going to have a bumpy ride."

And I don't say this to do that kind of disconnected false-pride thing. That thing where people label themselves as "fierce" or some such nonsense. I don't like that. It rings hollow. And I don't point it out to lay falsely low and feign a humility or a goodness that I don't feel and don't possess. Only to point out that acceptance of the self—of whatever we fundamentally are—is difficult. Acceptance of the wide swath of others? Perhaps more so.

We live in a world that preaches change as much as it preaches acceptance. Do I change? Or do I stay the same? Am I good enough? Or do I need to be better? And if the answer is somewhere in the middle—which intellectually I imagine is the case—where is that?

We live in a world on the brink of our extremes. Where the extreme example is the mainstream example. A world that is bright and shiny and glittery and horrifyingly accessible. A world where we complain that our children aren't as "tough" as we are, and yet we don't want the responsibility of the type of parenting which would create the kind of children we were.

When I am out at social functions, people often ask me about the experience of teaching. At a barbeque one Sunday, one of my friends asked me what the hardest part of teaching was. Before I could answer, he took a guess of his own, following up his question with, "Is it having to tell parents their child is different than everybody else?"

I answered, "No. The hardest part about teaching is having to tell parents their child is the same as everybody else."

My boss and I were once talking about the crises that some of our parents and our students face today. I am convinced it comes down to family size. When people had six, seven, eight children, they surely loved them all equally. But what they didn't have in equal measure was time. There was a notable lack of indulgence (which made us tougher human beings with amazing coping skills) . . . not because they loved us less, but because they didn't have, nor did they make, the time. They did not make the time for each child to require a different tone. The time for different consequences for different personalities. The time for each child to require a different dinner. And maybe that's okay, I'm not saying it's not. I'm not passing judgment on anyone. God knows if you stood in my shoes, you'd know I have no right to do so.

The point is.

The point is, I had the time. I sit here today, having had the time—only one child at home—and I didn't use my time well. I know a girl who we just pulled back from being way over her head on social media. And I saw it happening. I saw her withdrawal into a world I could not and cannot predict. I told myself that it was just the way kids are.

I saw her twitchy, almost narcotic-like, addiction to looking at her phone. And I shook my head. Indulgent. *These kids.*

I told myself that they need a little space and time to exercise independence. What is it we tell ourselves? We did stupid stuff too. We had even more time than they did completely free from our parents, and we turned out fine. They should have a measure of privacy as well.

But the difference.

Oh, the trouble is in the difference. The difference is that we are no longer in our world, are we? We've already established that on Facebook with all our "kids these days" lamentations. Our "if you grew up in the '80s" pats on the back. And they were great times, most of them. It's important to be proud, but we have to stop somewhere short of blind. Why would we apply the same rules to this generation? The same rules we abandoned? We've already changed the rules. We can't cling to the old days when life gets hairy, for we have not created the old days.

We changed the "old ways" because we didn't like them. We wanted to love our children better, more individually. We wanted to honor their learning styles, their personalities, their individual needs. And that came from a place of the greatest motivation. We wanted only the best for them. We wanted something better for them than what we had. And yet— sometimes I fear it has warped into a sad kind of negligence where we want to excuse ourselves from having to listen to tantrums and endure the uncomfortable responsibility of applying a consequence.

I sit on a fault line of sorts. My son in one generation, my daughter in another. Both had moments where they were in too far. That has defined teenage years since the beginning of time. But the difference is apparent. My son and I both entered the universe of the internet together. Sure, he was a natural at it sooner than I was because it was the language of his generation. It spoke to him immediately in a language that I could only hope to decode eventually. But . . . he was a user of it. Very much so. He turned it on, he turned it off.

Technology was accessible to him, and he accessed it at his convenience. But my daughter . . . it is in her veins. In her

DNA. In her bloodstream. It is a perceived necessity, and in many ways an addiction. It defies her free will. Look around you . . . it is an extension of every child and every parent. This . . . this world we all believe we control.

I have one rule around dinnertime at my house: no devices. That's all. I don't ask my children to help me prepare dinner. I don't ask them to help me set the table—and let me stop right here and tell you that it's because I'm a teacher. By dinnertime on any given day, what I want most is for kids to NOT talk to me. I also do not even ask them to clean up after: to do the dishes, to wash the table, to sweep the floor (see above reasoning). I don't even ask them to sit at the table until I am finished. We sit down, we pray, we eat. As soon as they are finished, and after they say "thank you" to the cook, they can leave the table. It has always been simple and a gloriously handy leverage for clearing their plates.

The only thing I ask in return is conversation. Tell me about your day. Look at me, a human being, and have some human interaction. Over time, they learned to like being known in that way. They learned to linger over table conversations. My son? He always understood this. Seamlessly. Flawlessly. To do this was an extension of him. My daughter? It was more difficult for her as her desire for social media replaced her desire for social reality at the table. Not impossible, but difficult. It began to take her longer to settle in. She knew the expectations, so she endured it gracefully, but it was very much not a relaxed feeling. Like she was kind of jonesing a bit through dinner. It made me sad, but I didn't address it.

It makes me sad to see the parent at St. Louis Bread Company who doesn't even look at her baby in the stroller. The kid screaming in rage because he has no idea how to cope with the relative boredom of the grocery store. It's like watching a ship sink. A sun set. The music die. This, the inability of children to endure through simple human interaction. And more and more, the inability of adults as well. How often do I occupy myself with being in a moment enough just so I can post about it? What is the narcotic effect of "likes" and comments that has us all salivating on the edge of all these attention-seeking behaviors?

I was in the store the other day, and a child was SCREAMING. Screaming bloody murder. I glanced up at a woman who was facing the situation (I had my back to the murder scene), and she glanced at me. She assessed the scene and said to me in a low voice, *"The kid wants the phone. Mom can't give it to him because her shopping list is on the phone, so she needs it."*

And yet. It's not fair to blame them, the children. It is not fair to them for us to abandon what we have created when it embarrasses us. When it looks foreign, rude, and unruly. It's not fair to throw up our hands and cling to "when I was a kid" statements and "back then" or "I told you so" when their road seems untenable and becomes unnavigable. It's not fair to shame their dependence on technology but then do nothing to change it. Never attempt to create situations when technology is not involved or not allowed.

Like the woman who eventually surrendered. Clearly mad and frustrated at her son, but she eventually gave up and gave him the phone. Saving face, she gave a little laugh as she did so. She smiled at me and said, "I hope I don't forget something important!" *Oh, honey*, I wanted to say. *You just did. The moment you handed over the phone you forgot something very, very important.*

There is a great quote that I can't formulate enough of to actually find . . . but on the fringes of my memory, it is about parents and ambivalence. Something about the defining characteristic of parenting being ambivalence rather than pride—because all parents know that at any moment, it could be the school principal calling their house to say that their child has just driven a car through the gymnasium—or something silly like that.

Look. The thing is. I don't know the answer. I have no clue what the answer is. I'm not a bad mom, and I cannot lay claim to being a good one either. What good would labels and blame do for any of us? I am only what I am in the moment I am in. And this moment? This realization? It's a hard one. We are all only parents struggling to find a happy medium in a world of extremes.

I have had to admit to myself that part of the reason I gave so much rope to this girl was because I did hope she would exhibit wisdom independently. I had faith in that. But my everlasting shame will be that when I suspected the faith was crumbling, I didn't check nearly enough, often enough. And the reason is no good one, no damn good at all. It was because I was scared too. I didn't want to know. I didn't want to know that she wasn't capable. It will always shame me a little bit that she was vulnerable with my blessing, and lost without my help.

As I began to reach out to other moms, I found so many disasters. So many near-catastrophes. So many war stories. It didn't make me feel better, but it made me feel not so alone. We are all in this fight together, and it's a war no one can win and nearly everyone is losing. I don't want to be alarmist, and the world doesn't need another extremist. God knows that solves nothing, even if human beings can't quite seem to grasp that.

Relationships are suffering. Children are in the wind. And we are only human, and perfectly balanced ones at that. We, too, have our brightness diminished by our fears. Our goodness masked by our cowardice.

I will only say this: First, forgive yourself. The goal of children around the world is to experience the world without the filter of their parents. Second, give them a little room—it is important to give them space to at least try to turn their own car around, and the opportunity to prove that. Thirdly, admit you are flawed enough to learn something—just as they are.

My takeaway was to tell Mags, "I want to always be able to trust you, but you are young. And young people aren't necessarily *un*trustworthy as much as they are *too* trustworthy. Of the world. Of social media. Of the perceived concept of privacy.

"So while I *can* trust you, I *will* trust you," I told her. "But I will trust myself the most. Trust my ability to monitor. Trust my ability to keep you safe. Trust my intuition when you seem 'off.' And when my intuition leads me to a place of worry, then we will follow my lead, not yours." End of story. Not a single question asked. "We will find a resting place until you are safe again."

36.

the good old days

In spring of 2014, on the heels of his graduation, Will asked me about my high school experience. It was a left field kind of question, and one that surprised me because Will was never impressed by the society of high school. I related some good times. The year our cheerleading squad and our soccer team won the Missouri State Championships on the same day . . . things like that. The highlights.

He said, "That must be one of your greatest memories." I looked at him, this dear boy who I suspected then—and I still suspect now—was experiencing an odd sense of loss for what he never had.

"It's a *good* memory," I corrected him. "It was a good thing to work hard for and be a part of . . . but it's not my *greatest* memory."

I added, "My moments with you and Maggie? Those are my greatest memories, they are my good old days, and your good old days are still to come as well."

Last week, on the way to her lacrosse practice, I related that bygone conversation to Maggie. Since she likes to spin out a thread of conversation, we went on to discuss the concept of "the good old days." Where it comes from, what they are, the memories they tend to be as dictated by society.

"But," I said, "what no one mentions is the magical thing about them." The magical thing about the good old days is that you are *always* a part of them. They are never gone. If not your own, then you are a part of someone else's. As you grow, you begin to have a role in the "good old days" of your children or your grandchildren.

I told her, "You never outlast the good old days because you are always in one part or another."

I am no longer on the stage, but I am in the audience. No longer am I the one leaving, but I am the one keeping the home fires burning. These, the "good old days," they are with us still. The wheel of life always unfurls something beautiful, evolving as we do. Always something new, always something old, always something good, always a new day.

Last night, Maggie attended my school concert with me, and then we went to Baskin Robbins for ice cream afterwards. Sitting at the ice cream shop along Main Street, we recalled how Nana and Papa used to call up randomly or stop by our house. "We're going to get ice cream," they'd say. "Do you want to join us?" And we would all pile in the car . . . our family of five. Who could resist the lure of ice cream with Grandma and Grandpa?

We sat on those old stone benches out front while the warm O'Fallon night settled in. She and I, chatting away. These days, Will is away at college. Nana and Papa have retired to Florida. But our life surrounds us still: her middle school up the road, the doctor's office right across the street. We repeat our favorite funny memories. We remember other dripping cones. Other summer nights like these.

"Remember when we were talking about the good old days last week?" she asked.

I had forgotten, but remembered again when she spoke of it. "Yes."

Then she gestured with her pink ice cream spoon—in one motion, she encompassed the moon, the night, the cones, the moment. The bells of Assumption Church rang out as if on cue.

"These are mine," she said. "I'll remember these."

37.

human-sized hearts

I'm very wrapped up lately in trying to release a little bit of crazy that has swung into my lane. It is never far from my mind, and I dislike it. The weight of it. I don't want it, them, that close. I want them to be as meaningful to me as the postman or a turtle dove. These people in our lives who pin our feathers.

The thing is, they've insulted a child in an effort to get my attention. A coward I could be called for not responding to the bait, but I would call it class. Dignity. Everything is turned inside out to fit a different mold. A surprising story. It is maddening. We are embattled. Oh not physically. But spiritually.

I have a beautiful life, and I only want to see beauty in it. But the tendrils of fear sneak in always. I want revenge. Wrath, it tempts me. And oh, I could rain wrath down upon them. Such accomplished martyrs. How do I release it? How do I root this from my heart? The toxins it has produced.

I should remember that the greatest blessing in my life is the love my children have for me. Surely that is a masterpiece. That Maggie can say to me, "Mom, I heard something about you . . ."

And I say, "I know that story well, and I could explain that to you, but I'm not going to." I could go on to say, "I will keep that story. I will keep all of its missing parts. I will carry the weight of the things you don't need to know." But I don't. I will leave words unsaid. I will shoulder the burden for love of her. So she can love who she deserves to love.

The burden is heavy. It is My Portion and My Cup. It is the price I pay for being wrong once. For wishing hope instead of despair. For once, long ago, living through the indignity of having to take an eye off one child to save the other.

Ten years have gone by, and the barb is still kept handy. What kind of person flings confetti around a person's darkest hour? God, I hope I've never done that. How they dance justice upon me, how they sharpen and aim. And yet, the beauty of my life is my love. That Maggie trusts me enough to believe when I give her no proof. To trust in the absence of an answer. I have to start remembering that no one can take from me what has been given freely. A child's love. A child's unwavering trust in whatever goodness I can claim.

"Mom," Will says, "your motherhood has never been in question. Not by anyone who matters." And they who matter number only two. They are holy and by my side.

Sue Monk Kidd once quoted in her book *The Mermaid Chair*, "Some say I fell from grace. They're being kind. I didn't fall, I dove." And there's a corner of my mouth that kicks up at the power of that. The fire and the disdain of it. But the fact is . . . long ago, I just fell. In defeat. Not grace, not anything courageous. I just fell in fear.

When you see your own child with wounds he has inflicted upon himself, believe me when I say you start screaming inside, a panicked hysteria that drowns out the world. That a terror will rip through your consciousness that will not be extinguished until you find a way to make their pain go away. And I thought . . . well, I thought it might take his pain away if we could start over. Someplace else. Someplace new. But I was wrong.

For years—nearly a decade—this taunt has been a feather in the cap of many. Some. And then only one or two. It was the muscle behind every jab, designed to inflict pain. It was the justification for every unkindness. The sentence that ended every conversation, the *coup de grâce* that negated my every input: *You abandoned your children. What do you know about parenting? About choice. About love.* And for years, I took these jabs. And oh were they plentiful. What, really, could I do? What right did I have to anything else?

"You weren't here!" I can remember the accusation. It reverberates in my memory to this day. The rawness of the voice. The fear of it, and possibly a hatred so well deserved.

"You weren't *here* when Maggie was crying on the bathroom floor last night for her mother, and YOU. WEREN'T. HERE."

And what could I say? I wasn't. Not in that one long-ago summer moment, I wasn't. What good would it do to grasp at the straws of my defense? I may have been unfairly judged, with a story never designed to be quite complete, but I was guilty nevertheless, of that I was certain.

And it's all jumbled. It's mistold. Misknown, deliberately misconstrued. Some parts left out, others rubbed to a high shine. But I have to remember that there is no glory in the high indulgence of wrath. There is nothing at the end of that road. No payoff that doesn't turn its thorns inward.

The truth is, what do I have to fear? My reputation? My reputation is genuine. It is not based on my success. Rather, it is rooted in what I have built upon my failures and shared for anyone who would be able to draw strength from them.

Ten years had gone by. The accusation had become disconnected, outdated, but was ever an arrow notched and ready: *You abandoned your children.* It quieted every defense, disarmed me every time. No mention, no measure was ever given for every lacrosse practice, every music concert, every soccer game that I sat, alone, on the sidelines. In the stands. In the seats. I didn't need credit, no. But how could anyone have missed the love I poured into every moment since?

Then one day, a moment of grace came, one whose glory belongs to God, not me. The same tone, the same words. But different because I was different. And suddenly, I saw what I had also missed in the ten intervening years: my own voice.

"You know, maybe you don't know this," I said. "Maybe I never told anyone . . . I know myself well enough to know that my silence on the subject is likely accurate. But my divorce coming on the heels of a son being so brutally bullied in school that he had begun to harm himself almost broke me. So, if I never said that to anyone—I am sorry. I'm *sorry* if I didn't take the time to make everybody *else* feel better. Maybe everyone needed to hear that."

I said, "And you can hate me for the rest of your life if you want to, if you *need to*, for the eight weeks when I was gone. Desperate, reeling in pain and confusion. Or you can forgive me for all the years I have been back. That is up to you. And I'm going to leave that with you from here on out." Then, like a gambler pushing all he has into the pot, I gave the anger back, and I forgave myself.

"Because you and I?" I said. "We are *never* having this conversation again."

It reminds me of an old fable about the wind and the sun competing to get a traveler to remove his coat. Some people in our lives—in all of our lives—are the wind in the fable, blowing and threatening. Freezing and forcing. I have been that, I have been the wind. And am I the sun in the fable this time around? Oh, heavens no. No, I am not that good. But I am not the wind anymore, and I have to hope that makes a difference.

I went out to eat last night with a dear friend of mine named Stacey. She, one of the only people in this life who would understand me clearly enough to say, "So, are you still processing? Nothing new?" Isn't friendship such a gift?

I said, "Oh, no. Nothing new. Phantom pains. Just the dregs of dodging this arrow yet again."

"For the millionth time," she completed my thought.

She always remembers how slowly and diligently I like to process things. Like a worker bee, tiny bits of progress. I want to package kernels of thought and earned wisdom in their proper spots. Stored in a healthy place so they can help build a strong foundation and not sting me later. Haste makes me nervous. For all my love affair with words, they don't magically fix anything. You can know something intellectually and yet never heal a wound.

We talked some more. Laughed some more at chaos and human foibles. At the end of one rosy-cheeks-margarita kind of laugh, I said, "Do you know? The more I discover, the more I realize, though, that I have to be nice."

She smiled and agreed. "Yes, you do. You have so much more in life."

Not in person. Oh, don't we all steer as clear as we can of our transgressors in real life? And that's okay, there is no reason to pretend as if no wrong has been done. From a safe distance, in my mind and in my heart, I can be kind. I absolutely must remember that these are the people we are called to treat with compassion.

There is an old Zen lesson about two monks and a woman which goes like this:

> *A senior monk and a junior monk were traveling together. At one point, they came to a river with a strong current. As the monks were preparing to cross the river, they saw a very young and beautiful woman also attempting to cross. The young woman asked if they could help her cross to the other side.*
>
> *The two monks glanced at one another because they had taken vows not to touch a woman.*
>
> *Then, without a word, the older monk picked up the woman, carried her across the river, placed her gently on the other side, and carried on his journey.*
>
> *The younger monk couldn't believe what had just happened. After rejoining his companion, he was speechless, and an hour passed without a word between them.*
>
> *Two more hours passed, then three. Finally, the younger monk could contain himself no longer and blurted out, "As monks, we are not permitted to touch a woman. How could you then carry that woman on your shoulders?"*
>
> *The older monk looked at him and replied, "Brother, I set her down on the other side of the river. Why are you still carrying her?"*

The thing is. It is disorienting to encounter souls out of time. Trapped in a place where we are no longer. On the surface, their grievances appear to be an angry swipe, and they are likely intended as such. But if you look at the undercurrent of the story, you see something much more cavernous and empty. These things from so long ago . . . to be still carrying them—enough that every snafu brings them fresh, raw, and roaring to the present—that is a story which is much sadder, much more worthy of compassion.

Some people in life can just be bloody awful. And yet. It doesn't give me the right to not do my best. I always tell my kids, "When you are standing at the gate in front of St. Peter, or whoever is holding the clipboard that day, you aren't going to be asked if you only bothered to do someone else's best. You are going to be asked if you always did your own."

I wondered a few days back, *How do you release?* And I have found in the meantime that it isn't anything grand at all. No monumental shift of understanding or design. Just one breath to the next. To remember that forgiveness isn't linear, it is cyclical.

I have to imagine it's enough to offer up the tangled knots of our experiences and tell God we are not able to fix it. To admit that we are not able enough to forgive the whole. I have come to realize over the years that is a story that runs both ways on a journey which is ongoing for us all. And I love the idea that God can hold onto it for a while and then give it back in human-sized parts for our human-sized hearts.

38.

the years between

A while ago, we were coming back from an event. It might have been Christmas. Maybe Thanksgiving. I said to Maggie from my vantage point in the passenger seat, "You should be at the Rec Plex."

And she replied very seriously, "I should."

This is a common thing we do. We enter the content of a passing billboard on the side of the highway into our conversation as if it's relevant. It's the same reason we stop all conversation and shout, "GOD IS FOR YOU!" when we pass a certain megachurch over in St. Peters. Because each windowpane of the church building contains one bold capital letter of this gigantic sentence.

Then, I can't remember which one of us said it first, but I looked at Dan, and one of us said, "You'd be home if you lived there."

"What?" Maggie looked around out her window. "Where does it say that?"

So we explained. There used to be a sign that said that at

some apartment building in North County, "The Old County" as I've taken to calling it instead of "The Old Country."

"Except I can't remember where it was . . ." I said to Dan.

He said, "It was over off Lucas and Hunt."

"Oh, yes! THAT'S where it was!"

A while back on the way to school one morning, I caught sight of a certain way I was holding my hands. And an odd moment for it to happen, but an old memory poked through. I told Mags, "After Dan had transferred to a different high school, a girl named Angie sat behind me in class . . ."

I can only assume the desk behind me was reserved for people who didn't want to pay attention in French class, because she would frequently "psssst" me from Dan's old seat and whisper-say,

"*MONA*. Look at my hands," and she would pose them just so, "do you think I should become a hand model?" And I would assure her that she did indeed have the perfect hand-model hands.

"Psssst! *MONA*," she would say when she got a new pair of flats—because she only ever wore flats, "Do you think I should be a shoe model?" And she would tippy-tap her toes, and I would assure her that her shoe-model game was strong.

It was always jarring to me whenever the likes of she or Dan wanted my attention. They were so larger than life. They were the beautiful people. It was like sitting in front of high school Beyoncé, and she needing your reassurance that she looked okay.

And while I know now that beauty is so much more than a face and, I imagine, to others I wasn't quite the level of bland I believed myself to be, my wisdom had not yet caught up to my life experience. So the attention at the time was as flattering as it was jarring. I related all of this in the car to Mags, then I related the contents of the car conversation to Dan at dinner last night.

I said, "Angie. Do you remember her? Tall, gorgeous? Always wore red lipstick? What was her last name?"

I shifted from speaking to him to talking to myself. "Angie? Angela . . . ? Bain? No, that's someone else. Angie . . . ? Harris? Angie Harris? Yes! Angela Harris!"

Dan still did not know the name, so I dragged out the yearbook. It currently holds the salad bowl at the perfect angle on my kitchen planters wall—and I only came by that happy information the other day when I was attempting to get the glass cookie jar down.

I flipped to the page and pointed to her. "Oh, yeah! I remember her," he said. "She was my buddy." And I'm sure she was. Dan was quite the connoisseur of the lovely back in the day.

"Nineteen ninety." I read the year on the cover of the yearbook he was currently digesting page by page. "Almost thirty years gone by." Where does the time go?

Maggie attributes the harmony between us to a shared youth. And, as I have said before, she is a little bit right, but a little bit wrong. By 1990, Dan had already come into my life and left it. Only to return twenty-five-odd years later.

There is such an enviable synchrony to being there in a life from the first. An enduring beauty to people who have spent the time from way-back-when together. To those who have navigated the thousands of ways life turns you from youth until now, and to have navigated that together is a thing so worthy of honor. Such a holy foundation. It is a steadiness I have never possessed. And that's okay. That wasn't my path to be on.

Dan and I share no firsts. Our past is only overlapped. We laugh that when he got sent out of French class, I was the one who had to walk him to the principal's office. But beyond that, we have few common experiences. But Maggie is right that we have many common memories. People, places. Moments in time. And that is enough.

On a rainy night, with the tires hissing on the pavement and street lights intermittently lighting our conversation when he can remember "Lucas and Hunt" for me, that is enough.

When I watch him flip the pages of an old, somewhat warped yearbook. He, now with black hair shot with silver and a back that bothers him from time to time after years of manual labor. When he looks at me now and remembers me then. That is enough.

When he reminds me that Village Square had go-karts. When I remind him that there has always been a mosque off North Hanley. When we both remember how good the sugar cookies at school were. That is enough.

It is a holy honor to be standing at the start. But it is an equally glorious gift to be the one standing at the end. To be the one who waits. Who collects the lines and ropes and strings and pieces of a journey lived so far. To inherit everything that's left from a life lived intentionally, sometimes recklessly, but always with great spirit and even greater hope. He who helps me to find, and to hold, and to be everything I have become in the years in between.

39.

still life

I have a plant in my garden. A blueberry plant. Some years ago, I wanted to try to grow berries. I thought to start with blueberries simply because I have friends who are blueberry farmers, and I imagined that their advice would be a good start. I bought two blueberry plants. One male (I think?) and one female.

As I placed these plants strategically within the profusion of the rest of my garden, I joked with my neighbors that I was setting them up on a blind date and hoped that one day they would find it desirable to reproduce. Which they never did.

One of them—let's say the male one—died. And the other did eventually as well. Or so I thought all that long summer. Come fall of that year, as I was thinning the garden, I snapped the twig off the male plant. It snapped. Cracked. Brittle. Broken.

But when I got to the other one . . . not so. While the appearance was exactly the same, there was still life in this one. And when I followed the branches down to the root, there was one green . . . thread. I wouldn't even call it a branch. It was green, and it was life, and it was about the width of upholstery thread and the length of a caterpillar. But.

Still life.

Some years back, I was struggling in my faith. How many of us have ever been in a situation where we were sharing our faith with people we didn't prefer. Sharing our faith with people whose chosen beliefs somehow did not mirror our own. Sharing a pew, and the Communion line, with people I didn't even want to share a conversation with, let alone an entire belief system. Where there had once been a fiery torch, there was now barely a flicker.

How many times are we in those relationships where once there was something and now it all feels so thin. Falling. Failing.

My friend Cathy once gave me the greatest relationship advice. She said, "Relationships are 100%. Every day they have to be 100% if you are in it to win it." She said, "But relationships are rarely 50/50. There are some days when you will have to come up with 90 because your partner has only got 10. There are some days when you can barely scrape together 15, and your partner has got to claw, and dig, and scrape to find 85 . . . because by the end of the day, the two of you have got to bring 100% to the table, together."

If you can do that, there is STILL LIFE.

When my mom and my stepdad Bill were trying to find the place where they wanted to retire, they searched a couple different places in the country. Arizona, California . . . and Florida was a rather late entry into the game. But it was Florida they chose in the end. When I asked her why, my mom said, "Because wherever we were in our lives at the time, and for whatever reason, when we went to Florida, I fell in love with Bill all over again. And I wanted to keep that feeling."

A thirty-year-old marriage. A brand-new, beautiful start.

There is STILL LIFE.

I went to 8 A.M. Mass this Sunday. I just took myself. That's one of my favorite things to do—to go to Mass by myself. No expectations. Nobody wants my attention. I think frequently about the 99% of this relationship that God does, and the 1% that I do. I hope I am grateful enough. I hope that I never forget to remember how much I have to be thankful for.

At the beginning of the spring, Dan asked me if I was going to pull the blueberry plant out of the ground, and I said no.

"Look!" I showed him the base of the plant. "There is still life left in it. I just want to give it a little more time."

He smiled as he does when he watches me pitter about in the garden.

"It's not doing anything, but it's not hurting anything either," I told him. In this, at least, I do 99%. The blueberry plant contributes a measly 1%. But.

There is STILL LIFE.

When I woke up today, I decided to pull that blueberry plant out of the ground. To heck with it! I had a tomato plant that needed a place to thrive. And my lemongrass planted from seed only *two weeks ago* is gorgeous and needs room to run. And this blueberry bush—

In the end, it is taking up valuable space. It has never contributed to the beauty of my garden, it has never borne fruit. It has stood leafless among the other plants of the garden for three years now. The thread of life I once saw has not reappeared. An abundant daylily keeps it company. Some plucky lemon thyme plays at its feet. And still nothing.

Sometimes, in some relationships, there is no life.

I brushed aside the daylily leaves and rooted through the thyme to unearth the blueberry plant. And there. There at the bottom: LIFE. But hidden. It had grown slowly in shade. It had used the shelter of those more vibrant to get strong again.

My Maggie had a hard year. Those of us who have lived through it know that seventh grade is the worst grade there is. The girls and the boys both are somehow, and for different reasons, the most unattractive versions of themselves. Not physically, no. It is their personalities that are so untried. They're so naïve. Their maturity is so disproportionate—body versus mind, boys versus girls, spirituality versus sexuality—that it is impossible as a parent to gauge who you are parenting today. The young woman or the child. The person who loves you or the person who hates herself. On any given day, at any given moment, this can change without warning. Everything is wrong, and then in a blink, everything is right. Emotionally, it is the equivalent of trying to stand with two feet in two different canoes.

But this summer—all summer—we took her phone. It was her dad's idea, and I hated it, but he stood his ground. I eventually agreed to the consequence, though not for the same reasons. He believed she would change her behavior if she feared the consequence enough; I believed she would change her behavior if we grew her *confidence* enough. In either case, we agreed that she had to go on a social media hiatus.

At first, it was brutal—like living with an addict. She was depressed, listless, angry. But then, she started to paint. She started to draw and read. In the complete *absence* of social media, her soul began to grow again. Through her own mistakes and through our intervention, she had been removed from a world that only cares for the physical, and she was allowed the freedom to flourish.

She admitted to me one day, "Mom, you can't imagine how fat I thought my face was when I looked in the mirror because all of the Snapchat filters thin your face down."

She said, "Now I can look at my face again and finally appreciate it." That was damage done only to a visual. Simply to a face. Can you imagine the damage that was invisible?

This summer, in the sun and in the wind, she has become an elemental being. She has breathed new life into herself. She has competed in swim meets at camp, she has cheered on her friends at track meets. She has been to sports camps. She is engaged, cheerful, and the loveliest she has ever been. She reads books. She has conversations. She is not OF the world, she is IN the world.

But like the blueberry plant, she grows under the canopy of us. We have sheltered her so that she could come back to real life. And like the blueberry plant, she will need to stand in the sun again. It is simply not practical that she never returns to the trappings of the modern world. She will soon have to brave the elements of her generation independently. But like the plant, I think she is stronger now. She can stand steady on her own roots. Stand up in the wind and the rain and know that she has the right to be exactly who she is and be proud of that.

Today in the garden, I did pull the blueberry plant out of the ground. It is ready to be in its own light. I have still put friends at its feet to steady the earth around it. And there is still much growing to do.

But blessed be the late bloomers. The life that grows a little differently. The little sprouts that take their time. And blessed be those who tend them. Those who wait out the lack of growth, who rejoice in a thread of progress, and who love when there is nothing pretty to see. Those who endure, who hope, who believe—even in darkness—that there is still life.

40.

in three days

Five days and one year ago, Maggie and I heard a little summer song on the radio. A windows down, beautiful little love song. Upon hearing the lyrics "I held your hair back when you were throwing up . . ." Maggie said, "Well, that is not romantic at all!" And I agreed that it was not.

But five days and one year ago, a little shell of a memory cracked open and began to germinate. Oh, not of throwing up. That would be ridiculous and untrue, but a memory began to put down roots nevertheless.

Four days and one year ago, I woke up to the memory still trying to tease itself forward. A party. Was it senior year? Perhaps some bad decisions, but what can I say? Homecoming queens have demons too.

But four days and one year ago, I remembered a night so long ago when someone (but who?) carried me up a set of stairs and into a safer place. Into a room, into a bed, where he found one of my girlfriends to take care of me the rest of the evening.

But really . . . *who was it*?

Three days and one year ago, I was lying in bed, a memory

fizzling out. Who really cares anyway? And I gave up the ghost and let myself drift off to sleep. But.

But three days and one year ago, in the hazy shade between asleep and awake, I remembered.

Snap!

I broke immediately to the surface of awake and said out loud to my empty room, "It was Dan Ford." And just as soon, I returned to sleep.

Two days and one year ago, I smiled when I woke up. *Dan Ford. Where is he now?* Gosh, I hadn't thought of him in a hundred years. Oh sure, we were friends on social media, but who is really friends with those people. Sure, some of them are, many in fact. But some of them, really, are just locked-in acquaintances. People we used to know. And maybe not even really then.

But two days and one year ago, I really needed a cup of coffee, so I got out of bed and forgot all about it.

One day and one year ago, I considered reaching out. *Was this you?* I imagined myself asking. I wanted to know because, truly, I had to know if my memory was faulty. And maybe it was. But maybe it wasn't. I was curious. And let's be honest, the years between fourteen and forty-four had treated him well. But one day and one year ago, I didn't have the nerve.

One year ago, I did it anyway.

I can remember the feeling. The pit in my stomach. The nerves in my fingertips. The sense that all this inanity was both necessary and uncalled for. Did I really need this man to answer this question? Oh, heck no. I know what I know. I know what I remember. And I remembered him.

There is a part of Elizabeth Gilbert's novel *Eat, Pray, Love* in which she attempts to describe the universe's way of drawing lives forward into other lives. Gilbert explains that she believes that the spirit of who you will become pulls your present self forward, sort of lights the path to get you from point A to point B.

I think of it in more faith-like terms. Sometimes a moment, or a connection, or a relationship, or an experience needs to happen. But there is no overlap, there is no reason these lives will ever cross again . . . and so the Spirit gives a little tug, a little Spirit shove, on the path. And just because the Spirit is grand doesn't mean the push will be. The spirit, the future spirit of you—these can only be determined by the relative humanness of you. And all the Spirit had to work with to get me on a path toward this man was a summer car ride, a song, and a girl saying, "Well, that is not romantic at all!"

Then suddenly, out of nothing, a match strike of a memory. A snap. A light in my path. But one year ago, he didn't respond. But one year ago tomorrow, he did.

He answered what we still call to this day "the silliest question ever": *Was it you who carried me up the steps that night?* An over-the-threshold-type carry, into a safer place? A better place than the one I was in at the time?

He said, "You know, I am sorry to say I don't remember. But I do remember me back then . . . so I know that just because I don't remember doesn't necessarily mean it didn't happen." Those darn demons, you see. They catch us all from time to time.

"But," he went on, "it does sound like something I would do." And it does.

I said, "Okay, thank you for answering. I know it was a

ridiculous question. Sorry to disrupt your life from thirty years in the past."

He said, "I'm glad you did. Reach out anytime."

A push. A match strike. A light.

I said, "Well, maybe I will."

And three days later, I did.

Three days ago, I said to him, "Did you know that three days from now, one year ago, I reached out to you and asked you the silliest question in the world?"

He said, "Has it been a year already?"

He hugged me tight in the vise that is him. Those whom he loves know this feeling well—he's strong and broad, and he throws all of his love into his squeezing.

I thought over our year: our first date at the farmers market, our first REAL date out to dinner, our first argument, the grace of our first forgivenesses. Will coming back from Japan, Maggie making her own missteps, the deer hitting the car, the bonfire when I accidentally might have burned his head a teensy bit. Our first Christmas, his first grandbaby being born . . . oh so much to be grateful for.

Then he kissed the top of my head. "It's been a great one."

I looked at him—this man who did indeed carry me to a better place—and said, "The best."

EPILOGUE

"Above all, keep loving each other earnestly,
since love covers a multitude of sins.
Show hospitality to one another without grumbling.
As each has received a gift, use it to serve one another."
~ 1 Peter 4:8-10

~ Witness, January 2013

Do I regret the pain I caused in 2008? I don't know if I can say. Do I regret the experience? No. Never. The experiences and the people opened up our world. Without them, our lives would lack so much vibrancy and I would be less of a person. Less of a mother. Less of a friend. Less of a self.

How can I regret that Maggie's sense of self is so linked to the sand and the waves and the sea? And Will's is so linked to the woods, the back roads, and the mountains. Perhaps I should regret that the uncertainty of that time was so stressful to Will that it might have been what finally broke him. But, no. Not even that. Because you should see him now. He has an amazing spirit of kindness and empathy. And if my choices were the straw that broke the camel's back, then the camel had been suffering under his burden for too long. Sometimes a person needs to break completely so they don't just walk around all the time dispensing the particular misery of the almost-broken.

And even to my own ears, that sounds self-satisfied. The truth is that I have never truly let go of the guilt. I have lived beyond it, and I have put good moments, better moments, between me and the brokenhearted me of way back then. The me that was too blind to see the boy and girl who needed me so much in every single moment. The me who didn't understand her own value to those two precious souls. But I will spend the rest of my life making it up to them.

The most I can say is that I tried to leave for Will and I came back for Maggie. Love, it is so painful sometimes. And it is the only thing worth doing well.

The years that followed were not easy. My life was not suddenly marvelous as Anna's was in Isle of Palms. *I had to learn forgiveness in all of its forms, how to live in both the presence of and the absence of it. And I had to find a way to hold onto myself while also healing the frayed edges of what I left behind.*

And to hear it now, maybe it sounds like I knew what I was doing. I didn't. Knowing what needs to be done and knowing what you are doing are not the same thing. I just kept my head down. Kept looking for the positives. And tried my very best to continue to do what I felt God was asking of me at any given time. And while I was busy doing that, God was busy as well. When I finally looked up from all my struggles, it was to find that He had cleared the rubbish and left me with only the things which brought me great joy.

For five summers, I lived on the Cape. Eventually, and as I had originally envisioned, we worked it out that the kids spend their time with their dad in Missouri in the summer and their time with me on the coast. I came home, yes. But I came home with the journey instead of leaving on one.

What I heard was a call to serve. To give back in any way I could, which never turned out to be very much in a capitalistic sense. But I like to hope it was, and continues to be, enough in a spiritual one.

My mom once said to me, "You have a gift. You can touch people. So many people move in and out of people's lives and are forgotten. But you are not. You are beloved." And while at times that has been a weight too cumbersome for me to carry gracefully, I now see it for the gift and the calling that it is.

I think we are each the main character in our own lives, and that is as it should be. You have a job to do while you are on this earth, and you better know that the work is yours. But it took me an exceptionally long time to realize that I wasn't only a character in my own life. I was a character in the lives of those around me.

Sometimes I had only one line. Sometimes I was an extra on the set, walking around in the background, valuable only for my reaction to the lives of those around me. In some people's lives, I'm an inspiration. In other people's lives, I am the antagonist. And in some lives, I am the heartbeat.

I am the mother.

I am the daughter.

I am the friend.

And people do *need me to* be *these things. Even if I think I am not very qualified for them. Even if I have been told so many times that I am no good at them and I start to believe it.*

St. John said right before he died, "Little children, love one another. If you do only this, it is enough." My job in this life is to love the people around me. To be a positive force in as many lives as I can touch. Katrina Kenison said in her book The Gift of an Ordinary Day, *"I so desperately want it to be said of me that I loved well." In the grand scope of a life, that is the only goal worth having to me.*

I still feel the call to leave sometimes. To live in other places. To meet people different than me. To expand my perspective and deepen my capacity for compassion, and that is as much for me as it is for my children. It is said, "Your children will be who you are, so be who you want them to be."

I want them to be filled with compassion. I want them to believe in leaps of faith. I want them to befriend the lonely, to understand the brokenhearted, to believe that goodness matters. And when the time comes for them to leave the safety of home, I want them to believe in the good they can do in the world. So, for them, I leave. I go before them and show them how it is done. And also for them I stay. So that, when the leaving is done and it's time to return, they have a place to come home to.

March 22, 1967

My Year of Silence

What I mean by my year of silence does not mean that I was stricken with the dreaded deafness of so many unfortunate people in the world; what I mean is something totally different to me and to so many more like me who were left speechless from a disease called cancer of the larynx.

Never will I forget that terrible silence and the despair I felt during the year after my operation. I never, at the time, realized what a wonderful feeling it would be to talk again. In fact, at the time, I had no idea at all that I could learn all over again with esophageal speech. This speech is mastered by long hours and practice of swallowing air and bringing it back up again. The belched air makes a sound which, with practice, can be formed very easily into one-syllable words. After a while a few words can be said together and finally you are able to speak whole sentences again.

It all started with a sort of hoarseness or huskiness in my voice which I naturally figured was a strain on my voice. I had to talk a great deal

since I was a bartender and met a lot of people day
in and day out. I took all kinds of lozenges, some
gave me relief so I forget about it and let it go on
and on.

By on and on I mean six or seven years. I did
nothing about it, which turned out to be the biggest
mistake of my life. When I finally went to a doctor
he recommended cobalt treatments, something like
x-rays only stronger. I started the treatments right
away, but no one knew that it was already too late. I
solemnly went day after day to receive the cobalts.

The treatments, even though started too late,
slowed down or stopped the cancer, but it did not
cure it. A few months later I was seriously stricken.
I was home alone, my wife and children out for a
ride that evening. I was watching television when
all of a sudden my breathing became labored,
[and] it got worse. I couldn't even reach and use
the phone to call someone. I had become desperate
for air and walked to the front door. At that time
my wife drove up and I collapsed on the floor. She
rushed me to the hospital where I was immediately
put under oxygen. My larynx had become so bad
that my air was being cut off and I was slowly
being strangled to death.

With the memory of this incident in my mind,
I was left with the decision of going through a
delicate operation or losing my life. This operation
would leave me with a hole in my neck through
which to breathe, since my nasal passages and air
passages in my throat would be sealed off. To me

this was a great decision, even though I knew there was only one answer.

The most agonizing thing about this was that I had six children in school and I was buying a house. I was trying to figure out what would happen to all of us.

The night before my operation these things were racing through my mind. I even thought that if I never came out of it at all, I would be better off. But that would be no solution at all for my wife and children; so I made up my mind then that I would conquer this terrible disease.

Two years have passed and I am writing this. I cannot begin to thank my family for being so brave and so good in seeing my anguish and despair while being speechless.

In the last year of my convalescence I have graduated from speech school and am now an instructor of esophageal speech at the Nu Voice Club in St. Louis, at the Cancer Society. I also completed my High School Equivalency course and have my Diploma. I attended M.B.T.I. and graduated with a Diploma in Data Processing. I am now in the process of getting a job in that field. It is turning out to be pretty hard for a beginner but one has to start somewhere to get experience.

I thank my Doctor, but my greatest thanks goes to God. I'll always cherish my second gift of speech and I will never forget my year of silence.

Henry Belgeri

CPSIA information can be obtained
at www.ICGtesting.com
Printed in the USA
FSHW011916040620
70865FS